the
BIGGEST
DAMNED
hat

Tales from Territorial Alaska Lawyers and Judges

the BIGGEST DAMNED hat

★ Pamela CRAVEZ

University of Alaska Press Fairbanks

Text © 2017 University of Alaska Press

Published by
University of Alaska Press
P.O. Box 756240
Fairbanks, AK 99775-6240

Cover and interior design by Kristina Kachele Design, llc.
Front cover images: Officials and members of Valdez Bar, Courthouse Feb 16, 1908. Pho-
tographer: P. S. Hunt, Photo No. G2911. Mary Whalrn Photograph Collection. UAF-1975-
84-462. (center) Detail from the courthouse in Valdez. UAF-1975-0043-00019. (bottom,
left)
Back cover images: Judge Arthur Noyes. UAF-1986-0033-00023n. (top). Grace Berg
Shiable. Anchorage Bar Association Oral History of Territorial Lawyers. Joint Archives
of the Alaska Court System and the Alaska Bar Association. (bottom)

Library of Congress Cataloging in Publication Data
Names: Cravez, Pamela, author.
Title: The biggest damned hat : tales of territorial Alaska lawyers and
judges / Pamela Cravez.
Description: Fairbanks : University of Alaska Press, 2017. | Includes
bibliographical references and index.
Identifiers: LCCN 2016031594 (print) | LCCN 2016031898 (ebook) |
ISBN 9781602233171 (pbk. : alk. paper) | ISBN 9781602233188 (ebook)
Subjects: LCSH: LawAlaskaHistory.
| LawyersAlaskaBiography.| LawAlaskaAnecdotes. | AlaskaHistory18671959.
Classification: LCC KFA1278.C729 2017 (print) | LCC KFA1278 (ebook) |
DDC 349.798dc23

LC record available at https://lccn.loc.gov/2016031594

To Glenn and our five-year plan to live in Alaska.

Contents

BIRTH & DEATH DATES FOR TERRITORIAL LAWYERS

James Wickersham (1857–1939)

George Grigsby (1874–1962)

Norman Banfield (1907–2000)

W.C. Arnold (1903–1989)

Dorothy Awes Haaland (1918–1996)

Mildred Hermann (1891–1964)

John Hellenthal (1915–1989)

Wendell Kay (1913–1986)

George Folta (1893–1955)

Seaborn Buckalew (1920–

James Fitzgerald (1920–2011)

Arthur David Talbot (1926–

Buell Nesbett (1910–1993)

Grace Berg Schaible (1925–

Russ Arnett (1927–2016)

Tom Stewart (1919–2007)

Introduction

When I came to Alaska in the early 1980s, Wendell Kay's name held a kind of magic. He'd be the lawyer you'd hire if things looked bad, really bad.

I only saw him once in court, toward the very end of his career, as he cross-examined a small female police officer who had made a traffic stop in one of Anchorage's wealthier neighborhoods. Kay, tall and silver haired, could have been the officer's grandfather. But he didn't play it that way. Instead, he became charming and interested in how she'd made this arrest, asking her question after question about where she'd been parked, the angle of her view, how often she'd parked in that alley waiting to arrest people, how often people rolled through this sign in this quiet neighborhood. The officer answered each, but the questions kept coming, time of day, amount of light, placement of trees on the street, and the officer's answers shortened. Kay continued, and let the officer's impatience surface.

Rolling through a stop sign is "failure to stop." And that's what this officer testified had happened. But laws are made by people and enforced by people, and if the jury thinks an officer is impatient for an arrest, trying to trap someone driving home from work, in a place known for people rolling through a stop sign, a jury might think there is something unfair about the situation. They might be looking for a way to give the driver the benefit of the doubt, and Wendell Kay obliges.

Kay, like many lawyers who came to Alaska while it was still a territory, became an expert at appealing to community norms over the law. Not surprising, since from the time of its purchase in 1867 to statehood in 1959, Alaskans developed a great skepticism of laws provided them. Commercial and government interests kept fish traps legal in Alaska while outlawed up and down the rest of the West Coast of Canada and the United States. The Jones Act required that only US-owned steamships could transport Alaskans as well as the goods needed to support their communities. Even after Congress provided Alaska with a territorial legislature in 1912, gold, salmon, and mining interests dominated the legislature much as oil after statehood.

More than most, Alaska's territorial lawyers understood the gap between laws provided Alaskans and what their communities were willing to enforce. For instance, Alaskans in fishing communities rarely convicted anyone accused of robbing a fish trap—or "fish piracy"— because of the general feeling that the law was unfair. Equally unfair to some was the requirement to pay federal taxes. Prior to statehood in 1959 Alaskans did not have the right to participate in presidential elections, leading Alaskans accused of tax evasion to successfully use the same defense that Patrick Henry invoked against Great Britain in the 1700s: no taxation without representation.

Although purchased in 1867, Alaska did not have a court on its soil until 1884. A couple of military posts handled problems. Congress dribbled laws, first a customs act, then part of a trade act, but no land laws, criminal laws, or civil laws. Anybody with a legal problem would have to travel to the US District Court in California, Oregon, or the territory of Washington to have their case heard. Not many made the trip.

In the early 1880s, Joe Juneau and Richard Harris discovered gold in southeast Alaska. Suddenly Congress became aware that Alaska didn't have enough of a legal system or laws. The Organic Act of 1884 provided a governor, one district judge in Sitka, a clerk of court, one marshal, four deputies, and four commissioners with duties similar to justice of the peace—all federal appointments. And Alaska had its first laws—well, Oregon had them first, since Congress extended the laws of Oregon to Alaska.

With the first court came Alaska's first lawyers. In 1896, even before the territory had its own civil and criminal code, Juneau lawyers organized their all-male Alaska Bar Association, requiring a dollar fee and adherence to a minimum fee schedule.

A second gold rush in Nome at the turn of the century brought two more federally appointed judges and a civil and criminal code. And more lawyers. Although the official count of paid Alaska Bar

Courthouse in Sitka, Alaska, circa 1880s–1890s. UAF-1981-192-00061.

Association members was forty-seven, a separate counting of Nome attorneys revealed 127 jurists in the gold rush city. By some accounts all it took was an oath in open court to uphold the law and a person could start advising clients and present cases.

Many of these early lawyers left Alaska. Others took over what would become Alaska's largest banks. Edward A. Rasmuson (father of Elmer and Evangeline) became head of the National Bank of Alaska and Warren Cuddy president of the First National Bank. Still others, like Charles Ingersoll, a successful hotelier in Ketchikan, turned to commercial ventures.

But some, both oblivious to and because of the unsettled nature of the law in territorial Alaska, stayed to practice. They used their wits and charm to persuade jurors. They learned how to deal with judges appointed through political patronage, often from outside Alaska and with little experience. And, they served in the territorial legislature and Constitutional Convention, helping to create territorial law and the constitutional framework for the state of Alaska.

In the early 1980s, the Anchorage Bar Association, having heard stories from lawyers about the territorial practice of law for years, supported an oral history of Alaska's territorial lawyers. As head of the project, I interviewed nearly fifty lawyers, including Alaska Supreme

Court justices, federal court judges, politicians, bankers, heads of law firms, and solo practitioners.

Their stories were tinted with nostalgia for a time long passed when lives were simpler and ambitions more easily realized. They remembered a bar where skills varied dramatically and allowances were made, where criminal trials were front-page news day in and day out, and where the court became a "jungle" where you never knew what would come at you since there were no rules of discovery.

Nearly every lawyer remarked upon the unique experiences Alaska offered, experiences they felt certain they could not duplicate—nor even had a desire to look for—outside Alaska.

They also remembered the murky, undefined lines between the personal, professional, and political. How the closeness of the legal community led not only to an ease of practice but also to mistrust and competition. The ultimate expression of this infighting occurred at the transition to statehood and has become known as the great Alaska court-bar fight, when the Alaska Bar Association sued Alaska's first Supreme Court.

My objective here is not to write an institutional history of the territorial bar but to capture something of its character. My method is to let lawyers tell their stories. Many chapters are based upon interviews I conducted with lawyers in the early 1980s. I've let them talk, so you can see their personalities and perspectives. Much of their concentration is on individuals who reveal themselves in some courtroom sleight of hand or some business blunder. As with all oral history, memories can be fickle when it comes to facts. You will get a feeling for the bar, including the privileges and prejudices of lawyers and their communities. You will also see the struggle between holding on to the frontier that brought so many to Alaska and the push toward statehood that would transform the practice, the legal system, and Alaska forever.

Although well-known during territorial years and in the early years of statehood, many of the lawyers you will read about have faded from memory. I confess to selecting stories from those I found most compelling in the ways in which they reveal both the era and community in which they practiced.

Norman Banfield, partner to one of Juneau's most successful lawyers, illuminates Juneau's legal hierarchy as he assesses his fellow 1930s practitioners. Buell Nesbett's command of a naval ship during World War

II seems a fitting preamble to his becoming the first chief justice of the Alaska Supreme Court.

There are two important events in which historical records are available and helpful. Chapters involving Judge Arthur Noyes' takeover of mining claims during the Nome gold rush and the Alaska court-bar fight rely on these sources. I've included historical and case law research in a few other places. You'll find the notes at the back of the book.

Sometimes, though, it's not the facts that are important. It's a gut feeling you have after hearing someone speak. I don't know how the trial where I watched Wendell Kay's cross-examination of the officer turned out. What I do remember is that every time I spoke with Wendell I felt his enthusiasm for the practice of law. He had an infectious energy that came through as he told stories about his trials. I'd gone to law school with no intention of practicing, but after hearing this man people called the "Silver Fox," I decided I'd try it out. I went to work in the Anchorage Public Defender office.

That was over thirty years ago. I could tell you stories, but I know they wouldn't be as good as the ones you're about to read.

1 ★
Three Lucky Swedes and One Corrupt Judge

Before the Nome gold rush, little about Alaska lawyers and judges caught anyone's attention. But in the summer of 1900, Judge Arthur Noyes stumbled into Nome with crooked lawyers and a political boss from the Dakotas. Together they set in motion one of the most infamous legal schemes to steal mining claims.

The story starts two years earlier, with three men, Jafet Lindeberg, John Brynteson, and Erik Lindblom, who within weeks of meeting one another discovered gold in a remote area on Alaska's northwest coast and set off the rush to Nome. Called the "Three Lucky Swedes," although one was Norwegian, their heritage became as important as their discovery in plots to relieve them of gold.

Lindeberg, the youngest at twenty-four, had left Norway in early 1898 to herd reindeer in Alaska. Tall and athletic, he contracted with the US government along with more than fifty Laplanders, Finns, and Norwegians. Upon arriving he traveled to the Seward Peninsula, where a small Scandinavian community had been established just sixty miles north of Nome. When the promised delivery of reindeer fell through, Lindeberg joined others scouring Alaska riverbeds for gold, hoping for riches like those found just a year earlier in the Klondike.

John Brynteson, born in Sweden, had spent more than a decade in the copper and iron mines of Upper Michigan before signing on to find coal for the Swedish Covenant mission on Norton Sound. With no coal to be found, the twenty-seven-year-old naturalized citizen began to look for gold.

Erik Lindblom, a naturalized citizen, though Swedish by birth, was much older than his partners. The forty-two-year-old tailor had been living in San Francisco with his wife and two children when he shipped off to Alaska and found his way to Council City.

In the summer of 1898, gold discoveries on the Seward Peninsula prompted miners to organize a mining district in Council City where they filed their claims. Lindeberg, Brynteson, and Lindblom found one another among the prospectors searching nearby streams and decided to set off together downriver to the coast of Norton Sound.

In mid-September, they loaded a flat-bottomed boat with supplies and began to search streams emptying into the Bering Sea. They traveled up the Snake River and saw a large rock that looked like an anvil standing above one of the tributaries. After inspecting the streambed, they staked it, claimed it, and named it Anvil Creek. Anvil Creek would become the most lucrative gold claim in Nome.

That fall, the three, along with other Scandinavians in the area who heard about the discovery, staked claims and formed the Cape Nome mining district. Dr. A. N. Kittleson, who had been the head of the Teller Reindeer Station where Lindeberg had originally been sent, became recorder for the district and registered the claims. After rivers froze, making mining impossible, miners set up camp and prepared for the spring.

News of the Nome discovery traveled fast. Unlike the Klondike where gold had been discovered a year earlier, and which required many miles of difficult overland travel, Nome, on the Bering Sea, was just a ship's passage from West Coast ports. All winter long people dreamed of the riches they would reap in Alaska, and made plans. During the spring and summer of 1899 more than 20,000 people flocked to Nome. They set up tents on the beaches, built saloons and dance halls, and crowded Nome's single muddy street, all hoping to find their fortune.

Disappointment met most who came for gold. Nome's most valuable parcels had been claimed, and the "three lucky Swedes," Lindeberg, Brynteson, and Lindblom, became targets of resentment.

Angry men, desperate not to leave Nome empty-handed, jumped claims, claiming ownership of the land for themselves. Some claims, it was reported, were jumped a dozen times. Some claim jumpers were

DISCOVERERS OF THE NOME GOLD FIELDS.
Jafet Lindeberg.
John Brynteson.   E. O. Lindblom.

"Three Lucky Swedes." P20-088 Alaska State Library, Alaska Purchase Centennial Commission Photo Collection.

paid off by original owners so that mining could resume. Others were not so easily dissuaded.

Lindeberg and his partners formed the Pioneer Mining Company as they drew thousands of dollars of gold from Anvil Creek claims daily. Guards kept claim jumpers at bay, ensuring work and assets remained protected.

By July, though, with the short mining season more than half over, rumors that Scandinavians could not legally own US land were proving irresistible. Although US law clearly provided ownership rights to non-citizens, the opposite had been repeated so often that hundreds of disgruntled miners agreed it must be true, and it suited their needs nicely. They called a miners' meeting—a formal meeting often governed by parliamentary rules of order, used by prospectors to resolve disputes.

Prior to the meeting, Dr. Kittleson, still the recorder for the district, alerted military officers stationed at St. Michaels. With tempers high and violence imminent, the officers charged with preserving order attended the meeting. When the vote was called to declare all of the Scandinavians' claims void, Lieutenant Spaulding interrupted and ordered the resolution withdrawn, threatening to "clear the hall" if the miners didn't acquiesce. Although not withdrawn, the lieutenant effectively made the motion to adjourn, "declared it carried and the meeting adjourned."

And then, everything changed. Gold was discovered on Nome's beaches.

Bars emptied, shops closed, and streets cleared as people sifted the sands for gold. Although there were greater gold rushes producing more money and more gold, none offered such an enticing prospect as Nome's beaches. By the end of the summer of 1899 the shores yielded $2 million worth of gold.

That fall, as winter closed in on Nome, the one judge appointed to serve all of Alaska, Judge Charles Johnson, traveled hundreds of miles from his post at Sitka to Nome. He ruled against those challenging the Scandinavians' claims, confirming that non-US citizens had the legal right to own land. Judge Johnson encouraged Nome citizens to organize their own government. They did, electing a mayor, city council, and chief of police—enough to maintain order among the hardy souls who would spend the winter of 1899 to 1900 in Nome.

As the days grew colder and shorter most of the 20,000 who'd come to Nome for the summer left on ships. The three lucky Swedes landed in Seattle with nearly $2 million in gold. They'd held the first claim jumpers at bay and had begun to see just how much they stood to make from their claims. They, however, were not the only observers of this great wealth. While Lindeberg, Brynteson, and Lindblom celebrated their success and planned for the next season, an elaborate plan was already in motion to relieve them of their gold.

Alexander McKenzie, Pepper and Son, St. Paul, Minnesota. State Historical Society of North Dakota.

Alexander McKenzie: Judge in One Pocket, Gold in the Other

Alexander McKenzie, dubbed "Alexander the Great" for his physical presence and political clout, entered Nome in the summer of 1900 and within days took over the Anvil Creek claims, leaving original owners tangled in a legal web. McKenzie never looked back, letting Nome lawyers and an unscrupulous judge handle the Scandinavians while he took the gold.

At six feet tall and over two hundred pounds, McKenzie had spent the past thirty years bullying his way to power, taking charge of people and situations to become one of the most influential Republican committeemen in the country. Born in Canada in 1850 or 1851, he left before learning to read and write and laid track for the Northern Pacific Railroad. Elected sheriff in the new town of Bismarck, North Dakota, he used his brute strength to maintain order. After six consecutive terms, he retired from law enforcement. Determined and ambitious, with a keen sense of opportunities and human vulnerabilities, McKenzie built a powerful network of friends and allies.

A political cartoon shows McKenzie sitting across the table from six men, each describing how they will deliver votes for an upcoming election. The contractor will deliver money, the chamber of commerce member will boost the price of grain just before the election, the harvester trust will have his agents and banker work for the ticket, and the railroad will guarantee all section hands' votes.

In 1899, at nearly fifty years old, McKenzie's accomplishments included engineering the transfer of North Dakota's capital to Bismarck, and selecting governors, state legislators, US representatives, and senators. With investments in real estate and public works, he'd put his weight into making North Dakota and its neighboring states fertile ground for large corporations and big business.

McKenzie bound his friends to him by "hoops of steel" and never forgave or forgot his opponents. Even after moving to St. Paul, Minnesota, he remained North Dakota's Republican national committeeman, his influence extending all the way to Republican President William McKinley.

Alexander McKenzie and "friends." Courtesy NDSU archives (NPL00052).

Observing the contested gold claims in Nome and the power vacuum in the new territory, McKenzie turned his efforts toward securing the gold for himself. He began by having Henry Clay Hansborough, senator from North Dakota, and Thomas Carter, senator from Montana, introduce language making "alien" ownership of land in Alaska illegal.

In the spring of 1900, mindful of the growing economic interest and inadequate laws and federal presence to provide order, Congress took steps to extend the civil and criminal codes of Oregon to Alaska. Although the Oregon code specifically allowed "aliens" to own land, Senator Hansborough and Senator Carter's amendment would change this.

Senators from other mining states blocked the amendment, concerned that it would open questions about ownership not just in Alaska, but elsewhere. They took action at the prompting of Charles Lane, a longtime California miner with an interest in the Nome claims. Lane, who had purchased a number of claims from Scandinavians in Nome in the summer of 1899, and invested heavily in developing his Alaska Wild Goose Mining Company, relied upon the original owners' legal rights to sell their claims. Lane's Wild Goose Mining Company and the "Lucky Swedes"' Pioneer Mining Company together held the valuable Anvil Creek claims.

Conceding that they would not be able to change the language of the law, Senators Hansborough and Carter took another tack. They persuaded their colleagues to delete all language concerning "alien" ownership. Here they had success.

With no language specifically allowing foreigners to own land in Alaska, lawyers were free to argue that the Scandinavians could not own the claims. Although a quick review of precedent would show alien ownership to be permitted throughout the country, a judge would be called upon to make this ruling.

McKenzie's next step was to recommend a judge for Nome who would interpret the laws for his benefit.

That winter Congress not only extended additional laws to Alaska, it also created two more federal judgeships, one for the area including Nome and another at Eagle, near the Canadian Klondike. McKenzie recommended Arthur H. Noyes for the Nome judgeship.

Judge Arthur Noyes.
UAF-1986-0033-00023n.

Judge Arthur Noyes: Providing Legal Cover

On paper, Arthur H. Noyes appeared well qualified for the Nome district court judgeship. Born in Wisconsin into a prominent family, Noyes was a Son of the American Revolution through his mother. His father had served as a captain in the Civil War and later became a respected lawyer in Baraboo, Wisconsin. Noyes and his brother received law degrees from the University of Wisconsin and began practicing law together in 1878. They moved to Grand Forks in the Dakota Territory in 1882, and five years later to Minneapolis and St. Paul. An active Republican, Elk, Mason, Shriner, and Knight Templar, Arthur Noyes was well known in the Minneapolis legal community. He and McKenzie had known each other for years and had many friends in common.

By the late 1890s, Noyes had seen a number of his legal partners gain appointments to prestigious judicial posts, including two district court judgeships for Minneapolis and chief justice of the North Dakota Supreme Court. He, too, had applied for a Minnesota judgeship, but was defeated.

When the Nome judgeship became available, Noyes not only had the qualifications necessary to be appointed judge, he also had the vulnerabilities that would make him a valuable asset to McKenzie. In addition to the recent defeat, he had drinking and money problems.

McKenzie spent thousands of dollars securing Noyes' appointment. He also secured appointments for the district attorney and US marshal. In July 1900, McKenzie traveled by ship to Nome with the coterie of court officials who would do his bidding.

The ship laid anchor outside of Nome on July 19, and McKenzie went ashore. He visited the law offices of Hubbard, Beeman, and Hume. The firm represented claim jumpers' cases and owned half interests in nearly one hundred claims. Hubbard was already well acquainted with McKenzie, having met him in Washington, DC. He'd hoped McKenzie's influence would be enough to change the law. When Congress failed to declare alien ownership illegal, Hubbard threw his lot in with McKenzie. Now McKenzie came to convince Hubbard's partners, Beeman and Hume, to sign over their interest in claims to him as well.

Within the day, Hubbard, Beeman, and Hume became shareholders in McKenzie's Alaska Gold Mining Company, a company he'd set up with capital stock of $15 million before arriving. The lawyers took leadership positions in the company and further entwined themselves in McKenzie's scheme by giving court officials a stake in their law firm.

With their interests aligned, McKenzie had the law firm draw up motions contesting ownership of the richest claims and asked the court to appoint McKenzie receiver while it decided ownership.

Before Judge Noyes opened court, McKenzie and the lawyer Hume presented the judge with all of the papers in his hotel room. When asked later why the motions were not properly filed and a summons issued to the other side, lawyer Hume told the court, "We could not find the clerk at that time. . . . Everything was in confusion then, and we simply left the papers with the court; that is all we could do."

On July 23, Noyes signed the orders making McKenzie receiver and requiring him to pay $5,000 bond for each claim, much less than just one day's yield from each. The judge ordered owners not to interfere with the receiver and that the gold should be preserved subject to further orders of the court.

With the judge's order in hand, McKenzie and a crew of hired laborers descended upon claims on Anvil Creek. Owners watched in outrage as McKenzie and his armed men took over their mining camps, confiscated gold, and started mining claims.

The Pioneer and Wild Goose Mining Companies on Anvil Creek had been producing tens of thousands of dollars' worth of gold daily. With McKenzie's men standing guard, the owners could not even see how much was being taken from them.

The next day, July 24, the owners provided proof of their ownership to Judge Noyes and asked that McKenzie be stopped from mining the claims. Noyes took the matter under advisement, stalling more than two weeks before denying the motions. With no other court in Alaska to appeal to, the original owners asked Judge Noyes, on August 14, for an order allowing an appeal to the Circuit Court of Appeals in San Francisco. The judge ruled that his order was not appealable. He then solidified McKenzie's position as receiver in a second order, giving McKenzie the power to take "all sluice boxes, dams, excavations, machinery, pipe, boarding houses, tents, buildings, safes, scales and all other personal property fixed or moveable . . . all gold, gold dust, precious metals, money, books of account, and each and all personal property" of all owners, employees, and anyone claiming a right to the property.

With Nome judge, lawyers, district attorney, and US Marshal promised a share from illegally mined claims, the "three lucky Swedes" had no hope of getting justice in Alaska's legal system.

Circuit Court of Appeals Reviews "Shocking Record"

The distance between Nome and San Francisco where the Circuit Court of Appeals sits is 3,000 miles. Each day of travel by ship between Nome and San Francisco, each day necessary to petition the court for hearing, each day the Circuit Court judge took to make a decision, each day required for the judge's order to travel by ship from San Francisco back to Nome, and each day that the order remained on ship outside Nome's harbor as stormy seas held it hostage represented thousands upon thousands of dollars of gold lifted from the land and into McKenzie's pockets.

The appellate court's order that McKenzie cease mining activities arrived on September 24, a full month after Judge Noyes' last denial. McKenzie had amassed a quarter of a million dollars in gold by then. Determined to continue, he ignored the order, claiming later that his lawyer had told him it was not enforceable.

Judge Noyes also tap-danced around the order, refusing to enforce it, and instead placed guards at the bank to "protect" the gold, which had the effect of keeping the rightful owners from taking it from McKenzie.

Finally, within a few days of the last ship leaving Nome for the winter, the California court dispatched two deputy marshals to arrest McKenzie. They transported him to California where he was jailed and sentenced to a year in prison.

The Circuit Court of Appeals' published opinion on Judge Noyes' rulings and Alexander McKenzie's actions came out in February 1901, long after mining ceased. The court reviewed Judge Noyes' "shocking record" and found all of the judge's orders blatantly illegal, bordering on fraudulent. Especially the appointment of a receiver to mine claims—that would have been better preserved by leaving them as is—and taking their only value. Although the court's original opinion stated that the owners had been restored all of their property, it was modified a day later with the observation that this was a "mistake of fact."

By the time the opinion came out, President McKinley had pardoned McKenzie due to his "poor health." Greatly recovered after his stint in jail, McKenzie returned to his political fiefdom and died twenty years later, a very wealthy man.

Noyes remained in office throughout the year under the cloud of McKenzie's unsavory influence. Although some attorneys enjoyed easy access to the judge and decisions in their favor, other attorneys found Noyes grossly incompetent and lobbied the president to have him replaced. Alaska's Governor John G. Brady feared reprisals against Noyes and requested he be transferred to Juneau. Juneau lawyers shot back that they had no desire for the judge to preside over their court. Finally, Noyes' presence was requested in Washington, DC. He boarded ship in the fall of 1901, reportedly in a drunken stupor with bags of gold concealed under his overcoat.

The circuit court found Noyes guilty of contempt, fined him $1,000, and removed him from office. He retreated to his home in Baraboo, Wisconsin, where he died that spring.

Classic Tale Captures Imaginations

Rex Beach might have become a lawyer if he hadn't decided to try his luck prospecting in Nome. The twenty-three-year-old had a couple of years of law school under his belt when he came to Nome the summer of 1900. Although he never found gold, he did see the McKenzie/Noyes story unfold, and it became his gold mine.

Beach wrote a nonfiction account for *Appleton's Booklovers Magazine* and then turned it into a novel, *The Spoilers*. The classic gold rush tale featured a political boss, a corrupt judge, a brave, young miner, and a love interest. Turned into a movie in 1914, it was remade in 1923, 1930, 1942, and 1955. In 1930, Gary Cooper played the courageous miner, and in 1942, John Wayne played the part.

The story captured the public's imagination and easily lulled people into thinking that Alaska drew only those interested in finding riches and leaving. There is, though, another side to Alaska's gold rush frontier, where personal and professional opportunities offered themselves to people who sought more than quick riches. The stories of those who stayed unfold from gold rush times forward, creating the legendary characters and personalities of Alaska's bench and bar.

2 ★

Wickersham Chafes UNDER EAGLE'S SLOW PACE

The two new judges who came to dispense justice in Alaska in 1900 could not have been more different, making Alaskans wonder each time a new judge was appointed, would it be a "Judge Noyes" or a "Judge Wickersham."

As Judge Noyes fulfilled his debt to Alexander McKenzie and helped loot the Anvil Creek claims, Judge James Wickersham presided over a sleepy post at Eagle in central Alaska and struggled to collect liquor license fees to build a courthouse. While Noyes ignored the Ninth Circuit Court, Wickersham tried to convince jurors to impose regular fines upon Eagle's houses of prostitution and gambling so there would be public money for a police force.

Wickersham, seeing his posting to Alaska as an opportunity to distinguish himself, chafed under the slow pace of his assigned post. When news of claim jumping at Rampart reached him, the judge hitched up his dogsled and traveled five hundred miles down the Yukon River in temperatures reaching fifty below zero to settle the matter. Called upon to take over the Nome caseload upon Judge Noyes' departure, Wickersham saw an opportunity to face the "greatest task so far in life," and "make a high and honorable record" as judge, he wrote in his diary on September 15, 1901. The enthusiasm with which Wickersham embraced his job at Nome typified his tenure in Alaska.

Born in 1857, Wickersham grew up in Illinois and studied in a law office before passing the bar exam. He took his wife and one-year-old

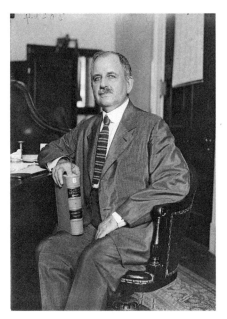

Judge James Wickersham.
Library of Congress, Prints and
Photographs Division, photograph
by Harris and Ewing, reproduction
number, LC-USZ62-123456.

Eagle Federal Courthouse built
in 1901 and used by Judge James
Wickersham. Library of Congress,
Prints and Photographs Division, AK,
19-EGL, 1-E-1.

son from Springfield, Illinois, to Tacoma, Washington, in 1883, lured westward with the expansion of the railroad to the coast. The move proved a mighty step backward in terms of civilized amenities but forward in terms of opportunity. Within a year Wickersham was elected county probate judge and later appointed city attorney.

Wickersham, politically active, understood how impropriety could hurt his career. His affair with a young woman in 1888 became the substance of a court case in which he was found guilty of seduction, a charge diffused only by the woman's later claims that she had

had intercourse with other men before Wickersham, and that her involvement with Wickersham had been designed to hurt him politically.

Still, the Sadie Brantner affair stalked him throughout his life. Opponents threatened to bring it up when Wickersham was nominated for the newly created district court judgeship at Eagle. The scandal did not prevent Wickersham from receiving the Alaska appointment, although he would have preferred the Japanese consulship for which he'd also been nominated. Once Wickersham accepted the district court judgeship, he made a lasting commitment to Alaska.

Clearing Nome's Docket

When Wickersham arrived in Nome in the fall of 1901, he found the city's legal affairs in total disarray. Cases were backed up, no decisions had been made for months, and the military was guarding the most valuable claims from jumpers. Miners, who had looked forward to the first court system for some stability and security for their ventures, were disenchanted and exasperated. Mining had come to a standstill for fear that any productivity would cause a challenge to the claim.

Wickersham quickly distinguished himself from Noyes, publicly declaring that he would tolerate no private communications from members of the bar. All of his decisions would be based on public arguments in court. He then went about clearing the docket, scheduling cases to be heard, and making decisions. In the following months he dealt with over four hundred cases: dismissing more than two hundred and trying the rest.

In July 1902 newly appointed Judge Alfred S. Moore took over at Nome, allowing Wickersham to go back to his post at Eagle. Less than a month after Wickersham's return, the discovery of gold by Felix Pedro, near present-day Fairbanks, touched off a rush to the interior where Wickersham served. For the next six years Wickersham presided over mining disputes, establishing himself as a just and fair arbiter.

Wickersham continued to thrive on the Alaskan outpost beyond gold rush years. In 1908 he successfully ran for Alaska's voteless congressional seat and served in that position for many years. Although this required him to travel to Washington, DC, Alaska remained his home.

Throughout his life Wickersham embraced the political and social challenges of the far north land. Somewhat restless in nature, he traveled extensively throughout Alaska, mounting an expedition to climb Mount McKinley and taking long dogsled trips to explore the hinterland. His abiding curiosity about the frontier resulted in a number of books: he edited the first Alaska legal casebook and wrote extensively on Alaska history, publishing his memoirs, *Old Yukon: Tales-Trails-Trials*, when he was eighty-one years old.

Legacy of Unpredictability

The two federal judges taking their seats in the far corners of Alaska in the summer of 1900—opposites in their response to the place—made it clear that frontier justice had as much to do with personality and character as it did with written law.

Judge Noyes, paid for and pocketed, relied upon the isolation of his post and the power of his position to bend the law to his benefactor's needs. Like many who came to Alaska, his goal was to make a fortune and leave.

Judge Wickersham settled in for a lifetime, drawn by a desire to serve and gain prominence among the small Alaskan community. He would never make much money, but instead leave his legacy in memoirs and law books, and with his wife's name on Mount Deborah, among the mountains surrounding the greatest mountain on the North American continent, Denali.

Judges Noyes and Wickersham set the bar—both high and low—for territorial judges to come. With each appointment to the bench Alaskans would question a judge's agenda, political debts, and long-held biases. They would wonder who might benefit and who might not.

Among those most interested in the answers to these questions were Alaska's territorial lawyers. Appearing day in and day out in court representing clients' interests, territorial lawyers became quick to gauge both the inclinations of judges and the interests of jurors. In the years to come, it would be lawyers, more than most, who would struggle against judges and their agendas and work to have a voice in their selection. But that would be far in the future. First, they would have some fun.

3 ★

George Grigsby's BIGGEST DAMNED HAT

George Grigsby never sat on the bench, never wrote any books, and never contributed to a body of legal scholarship. His accomplishments included a quick wit, the ability to tell a good story, and longevity. Arriving in Nome just as Wickersham was leaving in the summer of 1902, Grigsby's career spanned six decades, to the 1960s and statehood. His knack for treading the fine line between what was considered clever and what would be considered dishonest, made Grigsby popular and a very successful trial lawyer throughout Alaska. Lawyers came to court to watch Grigsby perform. Afterward they'd push back a few drinks with the old man of the bar and listen to him spin war stories. Impressions of Grigsby range from brilliant legal strategist to drunken bum, depending on where and when lawyers met him. But all pretty much agree that Grigsby represented, for good or poor, Alaska's frontier lawyer.

When twenty-eight-year-old George Grigsby first arrived in Nome, he saw beaches crowded with tents and streets overflowing with people. A familiar rush of excitement filled Grigsby, who had spent the past years traveling from mining camp to mining camp, from Cripple Creek and Victor, Colorado, to Butte, Montana, practicing law whenever he couldn't get by on hard rock mining. With Nome, he'd finally have the assurance of a government paycheck and an official position, while still not necessarily having to settle down. This probably crossed his father's mind as well when he arranged for George's appointment as assistant US attorney.

Young George Grigsby.
Joint Archives of the Alaska Court
System and the Alaska Bar Association.

Colonel Melvin Grigsby, no stranger to adventure or the advantages of political connections, had served in the Spanish-American War as the leader of his own regiment of rough riders. Friend and fellow cavalry officer, President Theodore Roosevelt, appointed Colonel Grigsby Nome's US attorney. The colonel advised the president that George would make an able assistant.

The confines of official posts didn't come easily to either Grigsby. The colonel, undeterred by the previous administrations' legal troubles and convinced he could make easy money on the side, cooked up his own deals with private clients, including Jafet Lindeberg and the Pioneer Mining Company. At least for Lindeberg, putting the US attorney on a $10,000 retainer for legal services was a small price to pay to assure business continued unimpeded by legal challenges.

Then, with winter approaching and private client business to attend to before the circuit court in San Francisco, the colonel decided there was no need for both he and his son to be holed up in Nome. He made George acting US attorney and took the last steamer out before ice blocked the harbor.

Practical Joker

George, unaccustomed to the scrutiny accompanying his public position or the need for propriety, liked to whoop it up with other members of the bar. Practical jokes at the expense of the judge did little to endear him to Noyes' successor, Alfred S. Moore. The assistant US attorney allegedly dared one member of the Nome bar to call the judge a "red-headed sonovabitch" to his face. The obliging lawyer, after much badgering, respectfully told Judge Moore, "There are people at the bar who call you a red-headed sonovabitch. I, of course, defend you."

Grigsby's youthful enthusiasm and lack of discipline took its toll on his office. He could privately boast of successfully convicting gamblers by "fixing juries," but a general feeling that Grigsby cut corners for his own purposes made him a liability to the judge. Judge Moore wanted his court to be above reproach, with no hint of scandal. When Grigsby failed to get a conviction in a high profile case, the assistant district attorney's cavalier treatment of the court and legal process came back to bite him.

The case involved the shooting of a police officer by the chief of police. Rumor had it that chief of police J. J. Jolley shot one of his officers because the officer threatened to expose the chief's protection scam. The chief allegedly extorted money from certain people to protect them from prosecution. At trial Chief Jolley presented an entirely different scenario. Jolley testified that he'd had to suspend the officer from the force for compromising himself by fooling around with a woman of the evening. Angered by the suspension, the officer threatened to kill Jolley. The two men met on Front Street. Jolley testified that the officer pulled a gun on him from across the street and Jolley shot first in self-defense. Jolley then shot the officer a few more times for good measure.

Grigsby prosecuted the case and the jury found Jolley not guilty.

The verdict caused a great deal of anger in the community, anger directed, in particular, at court officials who still didn't seem to provide justice. The grand jury decided to investigate. Three days after Jolley's acquittal a majority of the grand jurors condemned Grigsby and his underlings as deserving of "the severest criticism and condemnation." The grand jury charged Grigsby with aiding and abetting J. J. Jolley in committing the murder and found that Grigsby had shielded the accused throughout the proceeding.

In a direct reference to the Noyes court, the report said that the Jolley affair was "but a repetition of similar efforts that have been made in the past to shield criminal offenders who were able to render pecuniary or political services to a ring of as infamous plotters and plunderers as ever reigned in the darkest days of iniquity upon these bleak and barren shores."

While directing its wrath at Grigsby, the grand jury took particular care to support the judge, calling him "dignified and upright" and "a judge of unquestionable integrity, ability and fearlessness."

With this, the grand jury assured Nome citizens that their judge was honest and let the brash, young Grigsby take the fall for Jolley's acquittal. It is noteworthy that not all grand jurors agreed with the assessment. One dissenter was mayor of Nome and future territorial attorney general John Rustgard.

The truth of the grand jury findings—that Grigsby protected Jolley and engineered his acquittal—is less clear. What is clear is that the town needed to find blame for the apparent lack of justice and looked not to jurors, but to prosecutor or judge. Judges and prosecutors often influence grand juries, and Grigsby's run-ins with the judge and casual manner made him a likely target. The Jolley acquittal offered the perfect opportunity to publicly flay the assistant US attorney while praising the judge.

Then again, if Jolley was fixing cases, could one of his cohorts have been George Grigsby?

While Grigsby suffered public condemnation, his father had his own problems. Charges that the colonel left his post without permission and that he accepted a bribe of $10,000 from the Pioneer Mining Company pursued him. Aware that President Roosevelt could not come to his aid, Colonel Grigsby resigned.

George remained assistant US attorney until 1908, when he was promoted to US attorney. While Grigsby settled down, marrying Elizabeth Chapman in November of 1904 and siring four children, the community itself quieted.

After the first decade of the 1900s, the rush was over and Nome's population contracted to a neat 1,000 or so residents. With fewer and fewer people in the community, Grigsby easily shifted from one position of prominence to another. In addition to serving as assistant and US attorney, he worked as city attorney, and Nome citizens elected him mayor.

Success in Nome led Grigsby to try for higher office. He ran for delegate to Congress but failed to get the Democratic nomination. He did, however, win election in 1917 to become Alaska's first territorial attorney general and traveled to Juneau to take his position.

Penniless Poker and a Full Salary

Juneau, prospering from the operation of two gold mines and the newly established seat of the territorial legislature, offered Grigsby more opportunities to become involved in territorial politics and a back door to the post he'd sought earlier, delegate to Congress.

While working as territorial attorney general, Grigsby found time to work on political campaigns. When his friend and fellow Democrat Charles Sulzer decided to run for delegate to Congress, George rolled up his sleeves and hit the campaign trail, working hard to get Sulzer the democratic nomination. Using his rapier wit, Grigsby called one of Sulzer's opponents "a fine old lady with a 60-horsepower tongue and a mule-power brain."

Sulzer got the Democratic Party nomination. In the general election Sulzer faced the incumbent James Wickersham, formerly the judge at Fairbanks. The race was so close that a recount had to be done, with Sulzer ultimately victorious. It was a pyrrhic victory since Sulzer died before he could take office. When the Democratic Party held an election within its ranks to find a replacement, Grigsby skillfully maneuvered his way into Sulzer's spot and packed his bags for Washington. Meanwhile, Wickersham continued to contest the original election.

In Washington, Grigsby's reputation for being an amiable, although penniless, poker player remains of more note than anything he might have done in an official capacity as a voteless delegate. The contested election was finally decided in Wickersham's favor, but not before Grigsby served the entire term and collected full pay. Upon his return to Alaska, Grigsby seemed to tire of politics and decided instead to devote his time to practicing law. He turned to Ketchikan.

Finding the Biggest Damn Hat in Ketchikan

Ketchikan, throughout the 1920s and 1930s, served as the center of the fishing industry and a steady stream of legal work. Of particular concern to Ketchikan residents were fish traps, large semipermanent devices constructed of pilings and netting set at the mouths of bays to catch salmon returning to spawn. The traps provided a means of catching fish with extreme efficiency and minimal labor. Congress had outlawed the use of fish traps in the lower Pacific states but not in Alaska.

Attorney Robert Ziegler, interviewed in 1982, remembered stories from his father, A. H. Ziegler, who practiced law in Ketchikan in the 1920s. Anchorage Bar Association Oral History of Territorial Lawyers, Pamela Cravez. Joint archives of the Alaska Court System and the Alaska Bar Association.

Businessmen from outside of Alaska took advantage of this loophole, setting up traps and collecting their profits. Naturally, Alaskans fought the use of traps, but the canned salmon industry employed skillful lobbyists and attorneys to keep the territorial legislature from outlawing the devices. As a result, citizens took matters into their own hands and robbed traps. Criminal lawyers such as Grigsby could depend upon a share of the legal work generated by fisheries-related crimes, including, especially, the piracy of fish traps.

Prosecutors in fish piracy cases faced jurors who begrudged the salmon industry's stranglehold on their economy and major fishing sites. Prosecutors facing George Grigsby's clients suffered additional untold obstacles.

Alaska lawyer and state legislator Robert Ziegler's father, A. H. Ziegler, also an attorney, practiced law in Ketchikan in the 1920s. Robert Ziegler, when interviewed in 1982, remembered a story his father told him from the 1920s, when both A. H. and Grigsby practiced law in Ketchikan. Robert Ziegler eased into the story.

George Grigsby (second from left) in Juneau in 1935. Joint Archives of the Alaska Court System and the Alaska Bar Association.

The prosecution had a circumstantial case of fish piracy against Johnny Starkloff, a notorious pirate. The case rested upon an incriminating hat left at the scene of the crime. All during the trial the hat held a prominent position on the prosecutor's table, and it was apparent that the prosecution intended to connect Starkloff to the hat.

At the noon recess Grigsby went downtown to the local haberdashery and bought a hat of identical style—the biggest damn hat he could find. Grigsby got back to the courthouse before everyone else and exchanged hats. When the prosecutor called Starkloff to the stand and asked him whether the hat on the table was his, Starkloff replied that he had never had a hat like that in his life. The prosecutor confidently asked Starkloff that he just try on the hat. The hat came clear down to his shoulders and the case was laughed out of court.

Like many stories from territorial days, the story that Ziegler remembered from his father tells of conduct that would never be allowed in today's courts. But it also shows how territorial lawyers measured greatness. Grigsby's wit and calculated sense of how far he could go to win a case made him a legend.

As Juneau Rises, Grigsby Falters

In the 1930s Grigsby traveled back to Juneau. Gone was the informality of gold rush years.

Juneau's golden era, starting with the discovery of gold in 1880 and ending with the tax on gold and falling prices in the mid-1930s, served as the foundation for a carefully delineated society. Envoys from large salmon packing, mining, and steamship companies now traveled to Juneau, where the territorial legislature swayed to their demands and the city assured them of a secure foothold not to be found in any other Alaska city of the 1920s and 1930s.

For the savvy Juneau lawyer, serving outside interests paid well, with the only cost being that of maintaining professional decorum and discretion—not Grigsby's strengths.

Attorney John Hellenthal, interviewed in 1982, grew up in Juneau. His father and uncle practiced law there in the 1930s. John Hellenthal's memories of Grigsby from this time show the frontier lawyer in another light. "We used to have to put him to sleep in the cloakroom of the courthouse in Juneau on motion days," Hellenthal said. "He'd invariably show up drunk."

Whether Hellenthal's assessment provides a complete picture of the gold rush attorney during that time is unlikely. However, it does provide another view of Grigsby and may reflect the now-middle-aged Grigsby's inability to fit within what was becoming a more orderly legal establishment. Grigsby's criminal practice held less romance for Juneau lawyers. Now business-oriented firms serving national clients worked to match the professionalism of firms outside of Alaska. George Grigsby, the territory's first elected attorney general, served as a reminder of how far Juneau had come in the last fifteen years.

Anchorage Creates a Legend

It's no surprise that Grigsby left Juneau for Anchorage or that the legend of George Grigsby changes dramatically when remembered by Anchorage lawyers.

World War II transformed Anchorage, which until then had been a small town built to support construction of the railroad in 1915. During

Anchorage lawyers in 1949. *Back row standing, left to right:* Cecil Roley, Wendell Kay, Peter Kalamarides. *Back row sitting, left to right:* Daniel Cuddy, Stanley McCutcheon, Paul Robison, Herald Stringer, Edward Davis, Evander Smith. *Front row, left to right:* Harold Butcher, John Manders, George Grigsby, Dorothy Tyner, Warren Cuddy, William Olsen. Anchorage Bar Association Oral History of Territorial Lawyers. Joint archives of the Alaska Court System and the Alaska Bar Association.

the 1940s, when Grigsby began his Anchorage years, the town nearly tripled its population from 4,000 to 11,000. The building of the Alaska Highway, connecting Anchorage by road with the lower forty-eight states, and construction of military bases outside the city, created a boomtown. Setting foot in Anchorage, the sixty-six-year-old Grigsby felt the excitement of a restless city bursting at the seams. Hard drinking, random gunfire, unpaved streets, and opportunities beyond staid Juneau reminded Grigsby of the Alaska he'd traveled to nearly forty years earlier.

Grigsby teamed with Karl Drager, and the two wore a path from their office to court, handling motions and small civil matters—divorce, estate and contract problems, along with criminal cases, many assigned by the court. A good share of Anchorage's prostitutes relied on the talents of Grigsby and Drager to keep business from being interrupted by zealous prosecutors.

To young lawyers coming to Anchorage in the 1940s, Grigsby represented the bygone frontier era, the gold rush years. He won their admiration with his ease in the courtroom. This maverick attorney reflected how the Anchorage bar saw itself: sharp, wily, not overly concerned with legal technicalities, but wanting to win.

Lawyers discharged from the military and choosing to practice in Anchorage after the war had a particular fondness for Grigsby. Often they came to Alaska to escape the regimentation of the war years. They had seen the law become more technical as the tasks of government expanded and administrative law burgeoned, growing technocratic and bureaucratic. Young attorneys could look to Grigsby as a model for the life they sought in Alaska. Telling tales out of his many years in the territory, he became the head of the Anchorage bar, and in his seventies mentored a new generation of Alaska lawyers.

"There were an awful lot of young lawyers who admired Grigsby without knowing much about his background," John Hellenthal said in 1982. Hellenthal had also moved to Anchorage in the 1940s to cash in on the boom. Grigsby "kind of straightened up when he was much older. I guess he couldn't drink anymore. I liked to talk to him, everybody did, but I didn't admire the guy at all," Hellenthal added.

Harold Butcher, a close friend of Grigsby's in the 1950s and 1960s, remembered that Grigsby, once a heavy drinker, couldn't drink anything but beer when he knew him. "George would drink four or six 12-ounce bottles of beer a day—same as a couple of good stiff drinks," Butcher said when interviewed in 1982. Butcher, appointed to the Anchorage Superior Court bench in 1967, used to have lunch regularly with the elderly Grigsby.

Grigsby stories are legion among lawyers who started their Anchorage practices in the 1940s and 1950s. Sitting in the back of the courtroom, waiting for their cases to be heard, they'd watch Grigsby in action. The dozen or so lawyers in town were a close-knit group, meeting for drinks or lunch and trading war stories. It was at these gatherings that Grigsby legends stacked up one by one: Grigsby never wasted time on legal research, he could persuade the judge of his arguments without the law; Grigsby could take one glance at a case and grasp the legal doctrine intuitively.

Territorial lawyers who later in their careers would become state court judges bound by rules and procedures spoke fondly of Grigsby.

Grigsby personified a disappearing breed—the independent, creative practitioner unhampered by legal technicalities.

You Could Ask Grigsby Anything

Ralph Moody, later a conservative Anchorage Superior Court judge, remembered getting valuable help from Grigsby when he began to do trial work in the late 1940s.

Moody, interviewed in 1982, remembered when he had just gone into private practice after serving as an assistant US attorney for four years in the 1940s. Because of his trial experience, Judge Anthony Dimond appointed Moody to a criminal case. Moody's client, accused of robbing the newly opened Traveler's Inn and fitting the description of the robber, had been apprehended by the police when they found him hiding underneath a car. Money from the Traveler's Inn was also found on the man. The client explained to Moody that he was just a victim of circumstance. Having been in trouble with the law before, he had seen cops coming and dived underneath his car. Some other guy must have left the money behind, he explained.

The client changed his story a number of times and finally threatened him, Moody remembered. The client said that if Moody didn't discredit the prosecution's witness he would get on the stand and blast his attorney for not adequately defending him.

Apprehensive about being accused in open court by his client of being a poor attorney, Moody spoke with Grigsby. Grigsby told him to take the client's story, not comment on it. If the defendant blasted Moody on the stand the jury would return the verdict more quickly. Moody went back to his client and told him that if he took the stand he would probably be convicted. The client backed down and was convicted anyway.

Moody never forgot the sense of security he'd gotten from Grigsby's counsel. You could ask Grigsby anything, Moody said in the 1980s, and "he would tell you honestly, and no charge."

Frail and Fading

In 1958, with statehood fast approaching and more young lawyers coming into the territory, a few Anchorage lawyers got a tape recorder and sat down with Grigsby. Finally, they would preserve on tape the stories they had heard at every bar lunch, the tales from the gold rush, from

Juneau and Ketchikan, and even from Anchorage in the 1940s. After a lengthy session of prompting, head scratching, and not a little alcohol to induce the freer flow of stories, it became apparent that they had waited too long. The eighty-four-year-old Grigsby could no longer remember the incidents he had made famous.

A year later Alaska gained statehood, and a whole new group of lawyers came to take advantage of the opportunities available in the new state. To these young lawyers Grigsby was a relic from another age of opportunity. They saw him dozing in the law library or checking behind the 108th volume of the *Pacific Reporter* for the bottle of whiskey he kept there. Grigsby's frailty began to tarnish the glitter of his stories, now told by others. That year Grigsby left Alaska for Washington State, where he died not long after.

4 ★

Becoming Norman Banfield

When interviewed in 1982, Norman Banfield had been practicing law for nearly fifty years, making him one of Alaska's longest-practicing attorneys. Slight, mannerly, and chatty, he'd become accustomed to answering questions about the personalities and events that shaped Alaska's past. The seventy-five-year-old, a founding partner in Juneau's Faulkner Banfield law firm, had represented the biggest territorial industries: gold, steamship companies, and salmon packers. He'd been colleague, mentor, and friend to generations of lawyers, judges, politicians, and businessmen.

Sitting in his Juneau office on a bright sunny day, Banfield had an ease about him as he recounted story upon story of the small community of Juneau lawyers in the 1930s and 1940s. He showed a photo taken in 1935 of fifteen lawyers gathered at Grover Winn's cabin for a summer picnic. Banfield is sitting on a log with six other men. Among the row of standing lawyers is George Grigsby, directly behind Banfield. As Banfield held the photo, the time between the 1980s and 1930s slipped away. There he was in the photo, looking away from the camera, smiling as he listened to the lawyer next to him.

Staking Mining Claims: A Compatibility Test

Born in Cuba, Wisconsin, in 1907, Norman Banfield graduated from the University of Wisconsin the same year the stock market crashed, 1929. Although he got a job as a meteorologist with the Weather Bureau in

Norman Banfield. Anchorage Bar Association Oral History of Territorial Lawyers. Joint archives of the Alaska Court System and the Alaska Bar Association.

Washington, DC, bread lines made him concerned about his long-term prospects in the capital. When an opening with the Weather Bureau became available in Juneau, he took the transfer. Again, though, he found himself confronted by a tight economic situation.

By 1931 it had been a little over fifty years since Joseph Juneau and Richard T. Harris had discovered gold and founded the first town in Alaska. By the turn of the century Juneau's mining companies—which had consolidated into three major companies, the Treadwell, Alaska Gastineau, and the Alaska Juneau—provided a steady source of jobs and commerce and assured the small town a permanence unlike the boom and bust experienced by Nome and the Klondike. A commercial district, mining cabins and working residential area, a Native village on the waterfront, and the area of Chicken Ridge were developed. Chicken Ridge, probably named for the many ptarmigans in the area, became home to mining officials, doctors, lawyers, and many of Juneau's prominent citizens.

When Banfield arrived, Judge Wickersham was living on Chicken Ridge along with lawyers R. E. Robertson and H. L. Faulkner.

The Alaska Juneau and Treadwell Mines recovered more than $130 million and became the largest gold producers of low-grade ore in the world during their heyday. Although Treadwell had closed by the 1930s, the Alaska Juneau Mine still employed 650 to 700 miners and mill operators. The mine announced a $1 million profit in 1929.

Although the first division judge was to officially reside in Sitka, a courthouse was built in Juneau in 1893, eight years before the first division headquarters officially moved in 1901. The governor's house moved from Sitka to Juneau in 1906, and in 1912 Juneau became home to Alaska's territorial legislature. On Alaska's southern panhandle, with a mild maritime climate compared to the rest of Alaska, Juneau was a popular stopping-off place for those traveling to and from Alaska.

It didn't take Banfield long to realize that he'd have to make some changes in order to improve his financial situation. With Juneau prices five and sometimes ten times higher than those he paid in the nation's capital, his government salary of $150 a month didn't stretch far. Rather than pay a quarter for a shoeshine that had cost him no more than a nickel, or at most a dime, he bought Shineola and shined his own shoes.

Juneau courthouse, which in early years housed the jail on the lower level. P39-1018 Alaska State Library Case and Draper Photo Collection.

Instead of spending fifteen cents a day on the *Juneau Daily Empire*, he bought the Sunday edition of the *New York Times* for a quarter. When the Weather Service scheduled a pay cut for its employees because of the Depression, which, in this respect, had reached even Alaska, Banfield began to look for sunnier prospects.

At twenty-seven years old he already had the attention to detail and fastidious nature that those who worked with him in later years would observe. He'd carefully assessed where his skills might bring the greatest reward and in 1934 accepted an invitation to go on an expedition staking mining claims with one of Juneau's most prominent lawyers, Herbert Lionel (H. L.) Faulkner. It was a trip, Banfield said, to test the compatibility of the two men.

H. L. "Bert" Faulkner, one of Juneau's Chicken Ridge residents, had built a substantial legal practice. In nearly twenty years, the fifty-two-year-old Faulkner had amassed an impressive clientele of six mining companies; the electric, water, and telephone utilities; and one of the banks in Juneau. He handled these clients along with criminal appointments that all attorneys were expected to take from the district court. The substantive demands of such an extensive practice and the physical constraints of the 1930s—a case before the Supreme Court in Washington, DC, could take as long as twenty days between steamship and railroad travel—made Faulkner interested in looking for an associate. Faulkner's closest rival for legal business in Juneau, R. E. Robertson, had taken in a law school graduate, Alaska-bred Michael E. Monagle just a few years earlier to help with that firm's expansion. Faulkner, though, felt more comfortable with a man with no formal legal education whom he could mold to his liking—self-motivated, knowing the value of a dollar, ready to put in long hours. On his summer trek staking mining claims, Faulkner found just that man in Norman Banfield.

Although the Faulkner Banfield firm of the 1930s prided itself on providing a model of etiquette, decorum, and stability, Banfield tells stories of Bert Faulkner's early days and provides the firm's all-important link to Juneau and Alaska's rich past.

Faulkner: Police Chief, US Marshal, Lawyer

Like many who traveled to Alaska at the turn of the century, Bert Faulkner worked his way westward across the continent before settling in Juneau. Born in Nova Scotia in 1882, he completed high school there, worked in Boston and North Dakota, and eventually got a job with the Tongass Trading Company in Ketchikan in 1903.

In 1904, Faulkner was appointed police chief of Ketchikan, a coastal community of fewer than five hundred people. In 1907, Faulkner left for Juneau when appointed US deputy marshal and later marshal. Although Banfield did not mention it, these political appointments revealed Faulkner's early alliance and identification with Alaska Republicans. That Faulkner did not become a naturalized citizen until the 1920s did not affect his ability to hold office.

Old-timers remember tales of Faulkner helping arrest Robert Stroud in 1909. Stroud, who would later become known as the "Birdman of Alcatraz," was then an eighteen-year-old who had been pimping his girlfriend. When a client became unruly, Stroud killed the man. Faulkner was one of the first on the scene.

As police chief and marshal, Faulkner often dealt with lawyers assigned to his cases. He noticed many lawyers had less knowledge of the law than he had gained in law enforcement. Often lawyers started practicing after spending a nominal amount of time in the law offices of another equally untrained attorney. Realizing he could do better practicing the law than enforcing it, Faulkner edged his way into the legal profession. He spent evenings studying with Ketchikan hotelier and lawyer Charles Ingersoll, and later with Juneau lawyer Lewis P. Shackleford. With the election of Democratic President Woodrow Wilson in 1913, Republican Faulkner was forced out of his appointed post of marshal.

In 1914, Faulkner passed the bar and went into the full-time practice of law, taking every case that came his way. He took over Shackleford's practice and his main client, the Alaska Gastineau Mining Company. Through the years Faulkner would add many of the territory's mines to his list of clients, including Kennecott, Nome Dredging, United States Refining Company, Chichagoff Mining Company, Kensington Mines, Jualin Mines, and Alaska Juneau Mining Company.

Faulkner enjoyed telling the story from these early years of the successful defense he'd mounted for a client. And that he'd come to regret.

Faulkner convinced the jury that eyewitnesses had been lying when they said his client, Ettore Scataglini, had threatened another man with a sixteen-inch barreled revolver. It was very unlikely that a revolver would have a sixteen-inch barrel, he told the jury. And even if such an aberrant gun existed, it would be preposterous to think that anyone could carry it in a hip pocket, as the witnesses suggested. The jury agreed and acquitted Scataglini.

A few weeks after the trial Faulkner was talking with a gun store owner and the topic of a sixteen-inch barreled revolver came up. The store owner remembered having such a weapon in his stock, but told Faulkner he had sold it to Ettore Scataglini, Faulkner's client, a year earlier.

Faulkner, the ex-police chief and marshal, shared his courtroom success, with the caveat that his skill was wasted on a criminal client.

Faulkner and Banfield: Building a Business Practice

A year after starting with Faulkner, a year filled with eight-hour days and six-day work weeks, Banfield took the bar exam. The test was given by a three-member bar commission consisting of Henry Roden, Grover Winn, and R. E. Robertson. Two of the three examiners, Roden and Robertson, had, like Faulkner and Banfield, never attended law school. Although Banfield, by his own account, did not shine on the territorial bar exam, he figured the commissioners stretched the rules due to his partnership with Faulkner.

By the time Banfield passed the bar in 1935, Faulkner was shying away from criminal cases and taking only those the firm was obligated to take through court appointments. Faulkner had succeeded in establishing himself as a business lawyer, available to those needing help in their commercial, real estate, and other business transactions in Juneau. In the mid-1930s, those doing business in Alaska included the Morgan-Guggenheim syndicate. The syndicate had interests in mining, salmon, and also the Alaska Steamship Company. The Alaska salmon packers and Pacific Coast Steamship Company also had interests in Alaska. These companies relied upon federal laws that gave them a stranglehold on Alaska's natural resources and transportation. Federal laws included the right to use fish traps in Alaska, though they were outlawed along the rest of the West Coast of the United States. The Alaska Steamship Company and Pacific Coast Steamship Company benefited from the Jones Act, which required that all ships carrying passengers

Juneau lawyers gathered at Grover Winn's cabin in 1935. *Back row, left to right:* unknown, unknown, George Grigsby, R. E. Robertson, Howard Stabler, Hugh Wade, unknown, unknown. *Front row, left to right:* unknown, Norman Banfield, Grover Winn, unknown, Michael Monagle, unknown, unknown. Anchorage Bar Association Oral History of Territorial Lawyers. Joint archives of the Alaska Court System and the Alaska Bar Association.

and cargo from Alaska to the lower states must be built and operated by citizens of the United States.

For many years Faulkner registered as a lobbyist and representative of these interests. The firm would work to keep Alaska's territorial legislature from outlawing fish traps, regulating transportation, and levying taxes on these large commercial interests from outside of Alaska.

Representing national and multinational corporations provided both the Faulkner Banfield and Robertson Monagle firms with a certain prestige—even though many Alaskans were outraged that these corporations were taking Alaska resources and providing little to the territory in return.

The Faulkner Banfield firm capitalized on this aura of prestige, providing consistency in manner. The two men presented themselves as professionals in a community of fewer than 6,000 people. Always well dressed, precise, and with great attention to detail, they looked and acted like lawyers, even though they'd never set foot in a law school.

That both Faulkner and Banfield practiced with no formal legal education may not be tremendously significant in itself, but combined with the clientele they served—large salmon canning companies, the steamship company, and Guggenheim interests, all accustomed to hiring well-educated counsel—they demonstrated how "reputation" and "personality" could form the foundation of a thriving legal practice in Juneau, Alaska.

Although Faulkner and Banfield would have preferred not to devote time to criminal cases, it could not be avoided. The territorial court routinely assigned all attorneys in Juneau criminal cases.

Banfield remembered that criminal appointments could be costly to the firm since the territory only paid $25 regardless of the case assigned, and sometimes even that fee went unpaid when there was no money in the territorial coffers.

Decades after these appointments, Banfield recounted the costs to the firm of one court appointment, a retrial of a murder case that cost the firm over $3,500—not counting time that could have been spent profitably on other clients. Although Banfield didn't give the year or case name, he did provide a breakdown of the costs. The record had to be transcribed at $1,500, and the trip to appeal in San Francisco and the cost of two briefs printed in San Francisco added another $2,000 to the bill.

Much of Faulkner Banfield's business depended upon retainer clients, according to Banfield. Retainers ranged anywhere from $35 a month for a small concern to $200 a month for a salmon canning company. Out-of-town or other extra work added a charge to a regular retainer fee. Banfield also did a lot of probate and real estate work, charging $3 for a deed and $10 for a deed and a contract of sale. The $10 fee demanded quite a bit of work, remembered Banfield, including interviewing, collecting facts and descriptions, and drawing up the papers. The firm had no stenographer, just the two attorneys.

In the 1930s, the Faulkner Banfield and Robertson Monagle firms counted three-fourths of Juneau's businesses among their clients, excepting the Alaska Juneau Mine, which belonged to the Hellenthal brothers, Simon and Jack, according to Banfield. A vigorous rivalry existed between the two firms, with partners in each loyal to their own firm and clients divided.

Banfield Assesses the Competition for Juneau's Legal Business: Robertson Monagle

R. E. Robertson, like H. L. Faulkner, built his practice from scratch. A former court reporter, around 1911 he teamed with Royal Arch Gunnison, a former federal district court judge for Juneau and the First Division. The Gunnison Robertson pairing did not impress Banfield. The firm was much too willing to handle criminal cases, Banfield said. And the addition of Michael Monagle, who had a flair for the criminal cases and also happened to be a Roman Catholic in a town of mostly protestant northern European immigrants, did not improve the Robertson firm's reputation in Banfield's estimation.

Banfield, who naturally competed with the law school-trained Monagle, handily remembered a low point in Monagle's career. "It was one of those foolish things that people sometimes do. . . . Mike is really a very high class person . . . he [just] got sucked into that one," recalled Banfield about Monagle's suspension from practice.

According to Banfield, a man had come to Juneau and fallen in love with the daughter of a Juneau minister. Unfortunately, the man was already married and had to get a divorce before he could marry the woman. Monagle agreed to handle the divorce.

In those days, Banfield said, you had to have been a resident of the territory for two years for the court to have jurisdiction, and only the testimony of an independent witness could verify residency. Somehow Monagle got bamboozled into testifying to his client's residency, said Banfield, and suggested the conversation must have gone something like this: "Mike said, 'Well, I don't know, have I known you two years? I've seen you around here.' . . . [A]nd this guy sort of talked Mike into being a witness for him."

When the second marriage went sour, the upset minister checked into his son-in-law's past and discovered the man hadn't lived in Alaska the requisite two years. Monagle had to answer for his testimony, resulting in a suspension from practice.

Banfield, by the 1940s, completely identified himself as a successful corporate attorney. He noted that his firm built its clientele on a work ethic that embraced long hours and prudent billing. Small-town Juneau provided Banfield the opportunity to prosper during the Depression; to model a firm from the characteristics he held dear—thrift, hard work, and integrity; and to attain status in his community based on his achievements. Not all lawyers in Juneau shared Banfield's success at gauging community needs.

Solo Practitioners: They Lived, but Not Comfortably

While the two firms competed for a substantial portion of the legal business in Juneau, other Juneau lawyers handled general legal problems, including divorce work and real estate transactions. Banfield lumped Juneau's solo practitioners together: "They lived but they didn't live comfortably. I don't think the average lawyer in Juneau in 1945 took in over $600 a month," Banfield said.

Banfield, upon entering the military in the 1940s, remembered surprising the examining officer who asked how much Banfield was making a week. "I said, '$300 or $400 a week,' and he said, 'I said per week, not per month,' and I said, 'Well, that's what I make per week.'"

Juneau lawyers worked and lived within the radius of a few blocks. Friends, neighbors, fellow churchgoers, Elks, Masons, and rivals in court, they knew one another well. Banfield's assessment of his colleagues includes not only their handling of legal work, but his judgment of their personal affairs as well.

Henry Roden: Henpecked and on the Territorial Payroll

Although Henry Roden regularly served in the territorial legislature, had been elected attorney general for Alaska, authored Alaska's definitive mining code, and edited the 1933 Compiled Laws of Alaska, Banfield was not impressed. He considered Henry Roden's dependence on the territorial payroll indicative of his inability to survive on his own as a lawyer. Even worse, he was pushed around by his domineering wife.

Banfield illustrated his last point with an anecdote recalling Roden appearing in court while Roden's wife was sitting nearby as a spectator: "He insulted the court, I forget what it was," Banfield remembered. "The judge said, 'I'm going to take a five-minute recess, Mr. Roden, and when I come back I'll expect you to apologize to the court.'"

The judge left the courtroom and Mrs. Roden ran up to her husband and hissed, "Don't you do it."

"Henry knew if he apologized she'd probably beat up on him," Banfield said, adding, "Dinning in his ear all night."

Roden weighed his options and when the judge returned, told the judge that he couldn't apologize.

Banfield remembered the judge's response, "I'm going to fine you $100 for contempt of court. You will be confined to the jail until you pay it."

"Mrs. Roden wouldn't put up the money so they came around and wanted to take up a collection to bail Henry out. I didn't contribute anything to it," Banfield recalled.

For all his disparagement of Mrs. Roden's influence over her husband, Banfield recognized a kindred spirit. According to Banfield, Henry Roden never made money practicing law, having a hard time attracting private clients. If it wasn't for his wife's property they wouldn't have much. She controlled the purse strings and was a woman of great industry, taking charge of her property and Henry, when she could.

"If he did accumulate any money, in fact on two different occasions that I know of, not only did he put a little money into a venture, but he got his wife to put her money in. In both cases the thing went belly up," Banfield recalled.

Banfield remembered one particular occasion when Roden and his wife signed a note for $10,000 and Banfield had to collect on the note for the bank. He went to Henry a number of times to collect, with no success. "Ban, you don't know what it's like to go to bed at night and have that dinning in your ear hour after hour about how you got mixed up in this mining venture," Roden complained. Banfield responded, "Henry, the only way Alicia's going to forget about it is for you to pay it." Banfield collected.

George Grigsby: Wit Wasted on Clients

Banfield admired George Grigsby's ability as a trial lawyer, one of the territory's ablest. Sharp in court and on his feet, Grigsby rarely prepared for a case but relied upon being able to detect some weak spot in testimony and then to destroy the witness in an unmerciful grilling, Banfield recalled. But Grigsby's impish personality interfered with his practice.

Banfield remembered Grigsby cracking up solemn Juneau bar luncheons at Percy's Cafe with unmerciful comments about the federal judge, the US attorney, and his assistants. But, Banfield observed, his wit was wasted on clients. Clients don't want somebody who's witty; they want somebody who will shed a few tears for them.

Grigsby never made a killing with clients, Banfield said. He spent too much time turning his razor mind to lighter matters. He could never pass up an opportunity to play a practical joke, especially on someone as staid as Banfield's partner, Bert Faulkner.

Banfield remembered Grigsby coming into Faulkner's office and telling Faulkner that he was in a jam.

"Bert immediately suspected that the jam was financial," Banfield said, recalling the story.

"I got a chance to make some money this afternoon," Grigsby explained, "and I've got a little piddlin' divorce case in court. There's nothing to it, it's uncontested. Would you go up and take the lady into court and get her divorce?"

Faulkner agreed to help and went to court with the lady that afternoon.

"The judge leaned over to sign the divorce decree and asked Bert, 'When's the wedding?' Bert said, 'Pardon me, your honor?' And the judge repeated, 'When's the wedding?'"

"Well, Bert didn't know the lady from Adam. He had no idea who she might be marrying and wondered how the judge knew," Banfield said.

Faulkner went to get a certified copy of the decree and left the lady in the hall. He paid for the copy and when he got back to give it to her, she was gone.

"He looked down the hall and there was George and the lady going arm and arm into the US Commissioner's office to get married. George had to make some money that afternoon, that was his excuse.

"That's typically George. And he thinks that's a big joke on Bert. He could have had any lawyer in town do the same for him, but he just wanted Bert to have a story to tell," Banfield laughed.

Not only did wit weigh against a lawyer's success, according to Banfield, but so also did too great an involvement in politics.

"People who employed lawyers, and especially people who were particular about their work, were not attracted by politicians. It's like Milt Odom," Banfield said of the millionaire owner of Anchorage Cold Storage. "He called me up one day and wanted me to do something. He said, 'When can you do it?' and I said, 'This afternoon.' He said, 'By God, you're one lawyer that I can call up and he is in his office and he's not off on a political campaign.'"

William Paul, Alaska's First Native Attorney:
Public Relations Man

Banfield's critique of fellow practitioners Roden and Grigsby is mild compared to his dismissal of William Paul Sr., the first and only Alaska Native attorney practicing in Juneau from the 1920s through the 1940s. Paul, whose mother was Tlingit and Scottish and father Tlingit and French Canadian, was born in the Alaska Indian village of Tongass in 1884. Raised in a missionary school at Sitka and then at the Carlisle Indian Industrial School, a boarding school in Pennsylvania, Paul grew up learning English and white customs. He attributed his education at Carlisle with giving him the leadership tools he used throughout his life to support Alaska Native rights. He worked closely with the Alaska Native Brotherhood—an Alaska Native political organization established in 1912 to foster equality between Natives and whites. In the 1920s, Paul spearheaded the court fight for Native voting rights and became the first Alaska Native elected to the territorial legislature.

Public and private institutions in Juneau, like much of Alaska, discriminated against Natives during territorial years. Even after the legislature passed an equal rights bill in 1945, racial discrimination was endemic. Signs stating "No Natives" were common in the windows of restaurants and other businesses. Housing and employment were also restricted.

Paul's influence in Alaska's Native community resembled, in some respects, that of a political organizer. For those voters who could not read he would distribute mock ballots with cutouts so that they would know where to make their mark. Fear of Paul's power among Alaska Natives led the territorial legislature to pass a literacy law in 1925 aimed at limiting Native voting and undermining any political influence that Natives could wield.

However, the bill that passed included a clause that grandfathered-in Natives who had voted in previous elections, making it have little impact on Paul's voting base.

When the bill first came before the legislature, Faulkner—though not a legislator—had supported the literacy requirement, taking the position that "the right to vote was only the right to vote intelligently."

Banfield's assessment of Paul is harsh—and reflects both Banfield's prejudice and Paul's focus on politics rather than the careful management of his clients' funds. This tendency, according to Donald Mitchell, who wrote about Paul and events surrounding the Alaska Native Claims Settlement Act in his book *Sold American*, reflected Paul's inability to make enough money at his practice and other ventures to allow him to engage in the political activities to which he was best suited.

Those activities that Mitchell refers to as best suiting Paul included supporting the rights of Alaska Natives, including rights to vote, to own land, and access to equal education.

Banfield confined his assessment of Paul to his legal work, which he found deficient. "In the first place, he should not have been practicing law because he never read a law book, I don't think, after he got out of school [and] he never read one there," said Banfield.

Paul had more education, including more formal legal education, than Banfield. In addition to the Carlisle Indian Industrial School in Pennsylvania, Paul attended the Banks Business College in Philadelphia, Whitworth College in Spokane, and earned his law degree through the LaSalle University correspondence course.

"All he was, was a public relations man for the Natives, and he lived off them, and they got awfully tired of supporting him, but who else were they going to turn to?" Banfield said. "[Alaska Natives] always thought they had to be represented by a Native, and of course that was their trouble. If they'd only gotten somebody reliable, they would have collected their money . . . such clannishness ruined them," Banfield said.

Faulkner and Banfield represented Natives, but only on small matters. Paul "would represent them in criminal cases and he just wasn't qualified," Banfield said.

Juneau, like many small towns, considered those "best" at their profession to be those who made the most money and had the most influence, those who had lunch regularly with the judge and became exalted leaders in the Elks, and those who might have a house on Chicken Ridge. The privilege of being part of the white Protestant community in Juneau and attracting professional work and status through these associations would not be afforded William Paul.

Banfield recalled Paul's disbarment in 1937, after being charged with converting to his own account 2,000 cases of salmon he had received in a settlement for some Native clients. The disbarment came only after a three-man committee of Juneau attorneys convened to hear the charges. Paul did not appear at the committee hearing—perhaps believing it impossible to have a fair hearing—leaving only his wife and

Group portrait of the Paul family. *From left:* William Paul Jr., William Paul Sr., and Frederick Paul. P33-31 Alaska State Library Alaska Native Organizations Photo Collection.

attorney to come to his defense. Judge George F. Alexander, the First District Court judge in Juneau, reviewed the decision for disbarment.

Paul's "conduct in this case," Judge Alexander wrote, "besides showing a wanton disregard for the interests of his clients and of his duties and obligations as lawyer and an officer of this court, is rendered even more reprehensible by the fact this [sic] his victims, for the most part were Indians or natives, as we generally call them up here, and members of his own race, who looked to him with almost childish faith as one who could be implicitly trusted by them with their affairs; and their claims for the most part represented their entire seasons (or year's) earnings."

The court showed leniency toward Paul, providing that he could apply for reinstatement any time within one year after he had made amends and apologies to the clients done out of their money. Banfield recalled recommending, when Paul first approached the bar for reinstatement, that he be turned down. Paul was later readmitted and went on to handle much of the groundwork and follow up for the Alaska Native Claims Settlement Act (ANCSA). ANCSA would provide Alaska Natives with compensation for their lands and establish the Alaska Native Regional Corporations.

While Banfield dismissed William Paul Sr., he found his son, Frederick Paul, to be "a person with quite a little ability, and as far as I know has always done a good job. He was very active in representing the Natives in the Alaska Claims Settlement Act." Banfield remembered too, that he "earned a very substantial fee," which Banfield respected.

Simon Hellenthal: Defining the Law for Jury and Judge

The Hellenthal brothers were remarkable for their time; both graduated from the University of Michigan Law School prior to practicing law in Alaska. Jack Hellenthal arrived in Juneau in 1900, worked in Judge G. K. Delaney's law office, and by 1906 had become the attorney for the Treadwell Mine and later the Alaska Juneau Mine. His brother, Simon, joined him in practice in 1905, and together they built the Hellenthal Building in 1915 and continued the private practice of law. Also in 1915, John Simon Hellenthal, Simon Hellenthal's son, was born in Juneau. John Simon Hellenthal graduated from the Notre Dame Law School in 1939, continuing the family legal tradition. There were actually four lawyers among the first generation of Hellenthals to come to Alaska. A brother, Theodore, became a member of the Alaska bar in 1923 but did not practice and instead worked as a bookkeeper for the Treadwell Mine. A sister, Gertrude, taught school in Alaska. Gertrude left and went to law school, practicing for a short time in Illinois. Banfield observed that lawyers, like the Hellenthals, with too much legal education, could be at a disadvantage in territorial courts.

Simon Hellenthal, who would be appointed judge for the Third Judicial District in 1934, had a terrible time handling judges who didn't know the law as well as he, Banfield said.

Banfield remembered Hellenthal in trial telling the jury what the law was. The judge stopped him, advising the jury that Hellenthal was incorrect and that he should stop trying to tell the jury what the law was. Hellenthal turned to the jury and said, "Well, it was the law before your honor ruled."

The judge let Hellenthal finish the case then slapped him with a fine for contempt of court.

Always willing to help out one of its own, the Juneau bar took up a collection to pay Hellenthal's fine. "Let him pay his own fine," Faulkner told Banfield when the bar asked for his contribution. "He was disrespectful to the court no matter what the law was." And Banfield also refused to ante up.

The lack of skilled judges and an abundance of unschooled lawyers made for a peculiar justice system.

"No pre-trial hearing or anything like that," Banfield said. The only rules of evidence were the criminal rules of evidence and even then there were no special rules. "Whatever the judge thought the law was and whatever the jury decided" determined the outcome of a trial. If you had a judge who did not know the law, "you had to appeal to his common sense." If you made a reasonable argument, all right, but if it didn't sound reasonable to him, you were out of luck.

The lack of forewarning before lawyers went into court invited games. Banfield remembered one time, in particular, when this system of legal practice played to his advantage.

Banfield and John Hellenthal: A Contest of Wills

A very wealthy widow had married a doctor and set up a household with him in her hotel. The widow died and Dr. Palmer wanted a share of her estate, but her will left everything to her children. The doctor hired John Hellenthal to help him get part of the estate. Hellenthal, according to Banfield, assured the doctor that he was entitled to an estate by codicil—that is, he had the right to inherit the property he had used during his wife's lifetime. Hellenthal petitioned the court and Banfield, representing the children, opposed the motion.

With no discovery and no briefing, it was like a jungle, Banfield said. You didn't know what the other side planned to argue until you got to court.

Their day in court came and Banfield remembered Hellenthal making a big argument about how Dr. Palmer "devoted the last good years of his life to taking care of this woman, and then she left nothing to him, and that he was entitled to this estate by codicil." When Hellenthal finished, Banfield stood up. "Well, Judge, I don't have much to say, but the Legislature repealed that law on codicil last session. She died after the session ended."

"You just never know how a case is going to turn out," Banfield said. "No matter how good it looks."

Banfield didn't need a law school education to master the twists and turns of Juneau's legal practice. From the start, he and Faulkner made it a policy to know the judge—Faulkner played bridge with Judge George Alexander and socialized regularly with Judge George Folta. The two lawyers naturally garnered influence where it might benefit their clients.

The Faulkner Banfield and Robertson Monagle firms testified at the territorial legislature and worked to insure that the territory's laws supported their business clients' interests. With favorable laws in place, there was less need to worry about judicial rulings that could hurt clients.

The appointment in 1939 of New Dealer Ernest Gruening as governor of Alaska was a particular challenge to the Republican Banfield and his business clientele. Gruening, a tough, capable, Democratic politician from the East Coast, came to Alaska with the goal of preparing the territory for statehood. One of his first steps was to persuade the legislature to levy taxes on the wealthy companies that for years had been doing business in Alaska and taking their profits outside. Faulkner and Banfield, local counsel for many of these companies, found themselves in a pitched battle to preserve a whole host of laws that were embedded in the very foundation of Alaska's territorial legislature. The attempt to increase taxes failed.

No Suffering Fools

Banfield left Juneau to serve in the Signal Corps in 1942 in Anchorage. When he returned to Juneau, Faulkner was pushing sixty and Banfield took greater rein over the firm's growing stable of well-educated and talented lawyers.

For Norman Banfield, who weathered the Depression and flourished through practicing law in Juneau, the law was a business to be conducted with professionalism and order and always in service to the client.

Billing practices among law firms of the 1970s and 1980s caused him great concern. "They want to put down eight dollars for every telephone call that comes in. They spend half their time with big staff and $30,000 or $50,000 in computer machines keeping track of these charges. To me they're probably going to make more money, but I don't think it's good for the clients."

Although Banfield was not the most brilliant or accomplished of attorneys, according to Avrum Gross, who practiced with Banfield from 1960 to 1974, he set high standards for his firm and its dealings with cli-

Juneau bar circa late 1940s, early 1950s. R. E. Robertson (*back row, standing, second from left*). Robert Boochever (*back row standing, farthest right*). George Folta (*second row standing, first on left*). Norman Banfield (middle in light-colored jacket, *seated, fourth from right*). M. E. Monagle, on one knee, *second from left in first row*). Courtesy Richard C. Folta, "Of Bench and Bears: Alaska's Bear Hunting Judge," Great Northwest Publishing and Distributing, 1986.

ents. Banfield's attention to detail and integrity impressed Gross, who had edited the law review at the University of Michigan Law School before joining Banfield's firm and would after leaving the firm become attorney general for Alaska under Governor Jay Hammond.

Banfield's emphasis on charging only for hours worked also gave the firm a reputation for charging the least and making the most, Gross said. Which, he added, meant lawyers in the firm put in very long hours.

Banfield's perfectionism, though, created a tense work environment, and his flash temper could be set off by seemingly minor details. Gross remembered Banfield upbraiding partner Robert Boochever for his failure to line up the corners of a file. Boochever, who would be appointed to Alaska's Supreme Court in 1972 and in 1980 to the Ninth Circuit Court of Appeals, weathered Banfield's outburst, which occurred in the middle of the law office for all to hear.

Professionally, Banfield could be nasty and cutting, but on a personal level he demonstrated compassion and tolerance, Gross observed. Banfield, however, did not suffer fools, and, Gross added, there were a lot of fools practicing law in Juneau before statehood.

5 ★
W. C. Arnold:
Territorial
ALASKA'S
MOST
Powerful
Lobbyist

W. C. Arnold sat in a modern downtown Anchorage office behind an empty desk with an expansive view of the city. Nearly eighty years old when interviewed in 1982, he'd been Alaska's most well-known and powerful lawyer lobbyist during territorial years. Although pressed, he would speak little of his lobbying on behalf of salmon packing companies. He dwelled instead on his early years in Hyder, Alaska, before he became managing director of Alaska Salmon Industry, Inc. Arnold, courteous and formal as he listened to questions, was slow to answer and sometimes difficult to understand. Whether due to age, dislike of being recorded, or reluctance to talk about contentious issues and times long past, Arnold's story would be told more by others than himself.

Born in Walla Walla, Washington, in 1903, Winton C. "W. C." Arnold moved to Idaho and studied mining law for a year at the University of Idaho Law School in the early 1920s. By 1926 he had become discouraged with Depression-ravaged Idaho. A short stint in Idaho Republican Senator William E. Borah's office gave Arnold the idea of going to Alaska. Borah headed the committee in Congress that oversaw Alaska, and the senator provided Arnold with names of people who might be able to help the twenty-three-year-old find a job.

Arnold arrived in Juneau and used his political connection to get his first job: handyman and guard at the jail. It was the best active Republican and US Marshal Albert "Boss" White could do at the time.

W. C. Arnold. Anchorage Bar Association Oral History of Territorial Lawyers, Pamela Cravez. Joint archives of the Alaska Court System and the Alaska Bar Association.

But when gold was discovered at Hyder and the US commissioner's post opened up there, Judge Reed, cognizant of Arnold's personal recommendation from Senator Borah, appointed the twenty-four-year-old attorney to the post. Arnold could finally put his mining law education to use. Mining disputes were the most frequent issues before his court, which also heard small cases.

Arnold found relations between Canadians and Americans to be extremely cordial in Hyder, at the southern tip of southeastern Alaska, and its sister city, Stewart, just across the border in Canada. Arnold frequently crossed the Canadian border to socialize with mining personnel at Stewart and the more established Premier Mine. Each New Year's Eve, Arnold and his friends took horse-drawn sleighs over to Stewart, where the Canadian and American mining communities ushered in the New Year.

After two years, activity at Hyder slowed and Arnold was promoted to the commissioner's post at the more bustling community of Ketchikan, the center of southeast Alaska's fishing industry. As commissioner he handled minor legal affairs similar to justice of the peace, coroner, and magistrate.

Arnold could see that while gold could be an unsteady commodity, salmon provided a constant source of income for the territory. The entire physical and economic structure of Ketchikan rested on it, and Ketchikan was thriving. Fishermen's houses lined the shores of the town so that the men could go out of their front doors and onto their boats. While their husbands were out fishing, wives and children worked in the canneries. Arnold decided that Ketchikan's economy would not slow easily, as had Hyder's, and he scouted out a position in private practice.

When Ketchikan practitioner Lester Gore was appointed district judge for Nome in 1932, he turned his legal practice over to Arnold. A substantial practice by Ketchikan standards, Gore's business included representing the salmon industry on small matters.

Territorial attorney Burton Biss gave an example of how Arnold made sure his salmon clients were taken care of at the yearly hearings of the Department of Fish and Wildlife within the federal Department of the Interior. These hearings decided the time of opening of the fishing season and the particulars of the fishing regulations for that year. A fisherman's chance for a good catch depended on these rules. The aid of a good lawyer could make all the difference to the fishing industry, especially when those deciding a question were not well informed.

The issue of whether the crab season should be opened early or late provides a good example. The proponents of a later opening time would argue that if you open the season too early the crabs don't have a chance to fill out their shells and there is a great amount of waste. If you wait six weeks, the percentage of recoverable meat markedly increases. Those who wanted the season opened early argued that there is no discernable difference in the crab meat. But the real, underlying issue involved whether those with small boats got the crabs or those with larger outfits. If the season was opened too late the fishermen plied rough waters to get the crabs, which spent the summer migrating outward from the shallow waters near shore.

While Arnold took care of Gore's clientele, the salmon industry began to become more unified.

Salmon Cannery Interests Shape Alaska Law

Ever since the first salmon canneries were opened at Sitka and Klawock in 1878, investors from outside of Alaska had made provisions to ensure their continued profit there. They shipped in workers and supplies when it was hard to find local help at the prices companies would pay. By 1893, San Francisco interests controlled 90 percent of all Alaska canneries and established the Alaska Packer's Association to oversee their needs. Their lawyer, C. W. Dorr, not of Alaska, influenced Congress to pass some of the first laws aiding the packers.

The industry had its way with Alaskan law. The Organic Act of 1912 (the Second Organic Act) gave Alaskans their first territorial legislature. The act also forbade the territorial legislature from passing laws that would "alter, amend, modify or repeal any federal laws relating to the fisheries of Alaska." All power to regulate the salmon industry in Alaska, the largest industry in the territory and largest employer of Alaskans, was reserved first for Congress where Alaskan influence would be minimal. The White Act of 1924 gave the secretary of commerce the power to create fishing areas in any waters of the Alaska territory. Although outlawed along the western states and British Columbia, Congress allowed the use of fish traps in Alaska. Large semipermanent structures built to capture and hold large quantities of fish with minimal labor, these devices were opposed by many Alaskans who believed that they both cornered the fish market and limited employment in the industry. It took only one man to stand guard while fish swam into a trap. Forty percent of a year's catch was caught in this manner. Profligate use of fish traps contributed to exceptional salmon catches in the late 1930s.

In 1935, the territorial legislature by a vote of 24–1 adopted a memorial against fish traps, one of many such memorials that would be delivered to Congress in the coming years. A bill was introduced in Congress to abolish fish traps. Alaskans against fish traps sent their emissaries to the nation's capital. The salmon industry drummed up its own Alaskan support through "selective local purchases of supplies and insurance, legal retainers, and liberal placement of advertising." The bill failed.

In addition to opposition to fish traps, international unions fought the salmon industry's hiring of cheap foreign labor from the Philippines and the West Coast for duty in Alaska during the fishing season. Strikes hampered the packing companies.

In order to more effectively deal with these and other issues facing the salmon business, joint committees drawn from the Association of Pacific Fisheries, Northwest Salmon Canneries, and the Pacific Canned Salmon Brokers Association became more formal under the National Industrial Recovery Act (NIRA) as the Canned Salmon Industry. The CSI was legally allowed to set prices and production quotas. When the NIRA was declared unconstitutional, the CSI remained active but became less visible. In 1940 both CSI and a subsidiary, the Alaska Salmon Industry, incorporated.

Diverting Beer for Fish

In 1941, Arnold, already familiar with the yearly system of setting fishing regulations and handling one of the largest fishing clienteles in Ketchikan, became chair of the Salmon Consultant Committee to the US War Department. In 1942, he took over as managing director of the Alaska Salmon Industry, Inc. He negotiated all contracts between fishermen and packing companies, monitored all federal and territorial legislation affecting the salmon industry, and fielded lawsuits that might endanger the rights of the packing companies to have their fishermen in coastal waters.

In 1945, Arnold set up his headquarters in Seattle, but he scrupulously paid his ten-dollar lobbying fee and attended every Alaska legislative session for close to twenty years.

"Fish" Arnold, so he was known for his single-minded efforts, exerted so much pressure with his silver tongue and heavy pocketbook that he is still credited with killing basic tax reforms for those twenty years and keeping statehood from consideration for as long as possible. If Arnold ever made Alaskans angry, little of the anger remains. Those who felt his influence remembered him as a smooth operator who knew the weak links in the legislature and exploited them to his advantage.

Although Arnold did not speak of his lobbying days, his colleague, Norman Banfield—who worked closely with Arnold, since the Faulkner Banfield firm represented many of the salmon companies in various local matters—recalled this one.

It must be remembered, said Banfield as he set the scene, that missionaries dominated Alaska for years and easily persuaded Congress to pass a Bone Dry Law for the territory—prohibiting the sale of liquor. Everyone went to ingenious lengths to circumvent the law. "When I came in 1931 you could call up any taxicab and they'd deliver your booze," Banfield recalled. "The taxicabs were all Packards and they had extra springs in the back so they could put four or five cases in there." The extra springs were supposed to keep the car from looking too low slung and to hide the alcohol from prohibition agents. Eventually, the agents caught on and would stop Packards if the springs were down to normal, Banfield added.

In 1933 Congress allowed Alaskans "near beer." Banfield remembered that instead of the first legal shipment of beer going to a local retailer it went to a party for legislators thrown by Arnold and other lobbyists at the Elks Club.

Although not as unified as the canned salmon industry, the mining industry did have its Alaskan legal representatives, and many times its interests coincided with those of the salmon business. One of W. C. Arnold's strongest supporters in the territorial legislature was O. D. Cochran. Cochran, a practitioner in Nome from the very first years of the century and gold rush days and then later in Fairbanks, represented the United States Smelting, Refining, and Mining Company. For years Cochran was elected to the territorial legislature, where he did his best to serve the largest mining operation in the territory. Cochran rose in the territorial legislature hierarchy, reaching the posts of Speaker of the House and President of the Senate. With these offices he could make sure his mining company eluded strict legislative control.

Arnold never served in the territorial legislature; however, his influence—according to all those interviewed—was greater than several legislators combined.

6 ★

MILDRED Hermann and Dorothy HAALAND: Independent THINKING Women

Dorothy Awes Haaland, one of the first women to practice law in Alaska, sat in the living room of her modest south Anchorage home in 1982 and spoke about her work over the past decade traveling the state in support of passage of the Equal Rights Amendment to the US Constitution. "There are a lot of women in the professions that think, 'Well, I can make it. Why should I be bothered with the feminist movement?' I see the problems and if I can help those women that can't solve problems by themselves, why not do it? I think it helps all women, including me – although I'm certainly better off than most women."

By the 1980s, Haaland had been practicing law in Alaska for nearly 35 years. She'd served as a delegate to Alaska's Constitutional Convention, member of the last territorial legislature, former chief of the Anchorage attorney general's office and founder of the National Organization for Women in Alaska. White haired with horn-rimmed glasses framing slightly hooded eyes, she felt great relief when the feminist movement of the 1970s and 1980s finally put a name to the way she had always viewed the world and acted. "I'm sure independent thinking women were attracted to Alaska, especially in territorial days. While they didn't recognize themselves by that name they behaved as feminists and thought like feminists."

When Haaland was born in Minnesota in 1918, and while growing up in Cedar Rapids, Iowa, there were presumptions about what a woman could do with her life. "You were going to be a secretary, a teacher, or a nurse. They wouldn't even say, 'What do you want to be?'"

Dorothy Awes Haaland in 1955. UAF-1983-0185-00042.

Haaland decided to come to Alaska for the same reason she decided to go to law school in 1939: "I made up my mind that I was going to pick something I wanted to do whether everybody else thought it made sense or not."

In 1945, three years after graduating from the State University of Iowa Law School, Haaland arrived in Juneau with a job in the Office of Price Administration (OPA), the federal agency begun during World War II to compare prices and control rationing. There she met Mildred Robinson Hermann, head of the Office of Price Administration in Juneau and the only woman lawyer practicing in Alaska. Just the kind of woman Haaland had hoped to find.

Mildred Hermann: Peeved by Lawyer Lobbyists

Mildred Hermann, in her mid-fifties when Haaland met her in 1945, had been in Alaska for more than a quarter century and was well known in the community. Married to a local pharmacist, the mother of two teenage children, she'd become a lawyer in her forties "by accident."

Like many civic-minded women, she'd worked for years with the Alaska Federation of Women's Clubs to lobby the territorial legislature on behalf of women and children. As chair of the club's legislative committee, Hermann wrote an assessment of territorial legislators, including what they had and had not accomplished during each session. The popular review was carried in a special section of the newspaper with advertising revenues split between the paper and the Juneau Women's Club. The radio station gave Hermann free airtime, and many used the information at election times. But Hermann wasn't satisfied.

Heavyset, with a penchant for hats, Hermann used her physical presence, savvy sense of humor, and strong intellect to persuade. Ten years of teaching school had given her good experience handling difficult audiences. While working to get the territorial legislature to pass a community property law in 1929, Hermann got a "trifle peeved" when blocked by "the large group of lawyer lobbyists who at that session and every other session of the Alaska legislature . . . controlled legislation in the territory."

Two days after the session ended she registered to study law with a practicing attorney, giving notice of her intention to take the bar exam. At their next session, the territorial legislature changed the requirements necessary to take the exam. Now Hermann would have to either get a law degree from a law school—of which there were none in Alaska—or work for two years in a law office rather than just "study." When family finances permitted, she enrolled in the LaSalle Correspondence Law School program and successfully completed it. She applied to take the territorial bar exam, and in August 1935—after being required to take the exam more than once—Hermann became a member of the Alaska bar.

According to Juneau Superior Court Judge Thomas "Tom" Stewart, who later worked with Hermann, law examiners were reluctant to admit a woman to the bar. Norman Banfield contended Hermann's law degree and education from a "correspondence course" were substandard. Whatever the reasons for delay, Hermann finally broke into the all-male Alaska bar.

Hermann spoke about being the only woman lawyer in Alaska at a luncheon of the Women's Bar Association of Illinois in 1939. A year later, an article by Hermann appeared in the *Women's Law Journal*, a national publication. In the article, Hermann is lighthearted, positive, and smart. She never takes herself too seriously and deflects any sense of grand ambition.

Mildred Hermann at the time of the 1955 Constitutional Convention. Joint archives of the Alaska Court System and Alaska Bar Association.

She'd never really intended to practice law, she wrote. "If I thought about the matter at all it was with the feeling that this was a man's country and a woman would have no chance breaking into a man's field." Yet a week after the newspaper announced her admission to the bar, her first client walked through the door; she had been practicing ever since.

As for her male colleagues, she found them to demonstrate good sportsmanship and courtesy. She singled out the Hellenthal and Hellenthal firm as being especially helpful, which would have pleased her audience, since Jack and Simon Hellenthal's sister, Gertrude, was a member of the Illinois bar and well known to the women.

Her national audience did not hear her opinion of Norman Banfield, who began to practice law at the same time as she. Nor did she write of other lawyers among the "lawyer lobby." That she'd gotten her law degree to level the playing field with them was all that counted. And now that the playing field had been leveled, she made it her own. The female lawyers who heard Hermann talk responded in a similar double-speak that remained positive, leaving the negative to be read between the lines.

From Mrs. Herman's [*sic*] account of her success as a lawyer almost from the day of her admission to the bar of Alaska, and the trek of clients to hers as well as to Juneau law offices in general, many lawyers in all the large cities throughout the country might turn green with envy. In fact, listening to Mrs. Herman, many lawyers might be spurred on to kick the dust off their shoes in these lawyer-crowded places where, 'tis said, one cannot drop a book out of a window without striking at least three lawyers, and make a beeline for that great territory.

Rosy Picture or Reality?

Whether Hermann painted an overly rosy picture of her legal practice is open to debate. That it would be easier for a woman to practice law in Alaska than in a large city was probably true.

Most law schools took few women, and those who did graduate and pass the bar found little opportunity beyond practicing with husbands and family members, as clerks to other lawyers, stenographers in law offices, in bureaucratic positions, or working in areas such as domestic and child welfare. Dorothy Haaland's law school class of 1942 had five women among one hundred men. The number of women was larger than the one or two usually admitted because most men were being drawn into the war effort. Haaland began her career with the Office of Price Administration in Washington, DC, a bureaucratic position, then "kicked the dust off her shoes" and transferred to Alaska. If she'd wanted to practice in a law firm—either in a big city or in Alaska—her choices would be limited and chances of partnership slim to none. But Alaska would offer Haaland different opportunities as a female lawyer than she'd have had elsewhere.

Alaska's small population and remote nature gave women—at least white women—more avenues to participate in civic affairs than much of the rest of the country. The first territorial legislature (all male) granted women the right to vote in 1913, seven years before passage of the Nineteenth Amendment in 1920. Alaska women had the right to sit on juries in 1923, making it easier to convene juries. Only nineteen states called women to serve on juries in 1923. These included Arkansas, California, Delaware, Indiana, Iowa, Kansas, Kentucky, Louisiana, Maine, Michigan, Minnesota, Nevada, New Jersey, North Dakota, Ohio, Oregon, Pennsylvania, Washington, and Wisconsin. Women were eligible to serve in Utah but were exempted, so they did not sit on juries. There were twenty-nine states that did not allow women to sit on juries. It would be more than thirty years before women would have the right to sit on federal juries and more than fifty years before the Supreme Court held the exclusion of women from juries to be impermissible in 1975.

Alaska's Earliest Female Lawyers

Although there were no female lawyers practicing when Mildred Hermann entered the Alaska bar in Juneau, there are historical references to at least three women admitted to the Alaska bar prior to the 1930s. There could easily be more that have yet to be discovered among historical files.

Nathalena Roberts Moore: Washington and Alaska Lawyer

Nathalena "Natalie" Roberts could very well be the first woman admitted to the Alaska bar. Born in 1875 in Essex, Massachusetts, Roberts grew up in Tacoma, Washington, with her mother. She attended the Annie Wright Seminary in Tacoma and then studied law with attorneys Boyle and Richardson. In 1899, at twenty-four years old, Roberts passed the Washington bar examination and was admitted to practice four years later.

Roberts practiced law and worked for the Northern Pacific Railway as chief clerk in the legal department. About 1905, she traveled to Fairbanks and began to work as a stenographer, first in the law offices of Carr and Nye and later with McGinn and Sullivan.

Fairbanks in 1905 had about 5,000 people, making it one of Alaska's largest communities. Gold production from nearby mines reached $6 million in 1906. Unlike Nome, Fairbanks' gold was farther underground, requiring more perseverance. By the time Roberts arrived there was a school, hospital, and a number of churches along with the other trappings of Alaska's frontier towns including prostitution, gambling, and round-the-clock saloons.

Roberts married Fairbanks dentist Charles Merton Moore and, in 1908, was admitted to the Alaska bar through reciprocity upon the recommendation of Judge James Wickersham.

Reciprocity allows an attorney, who has passed the bar in one state, to practice in another upon motion and without taking the bar exam. Each state has its own rules of reciprocity.

Natalie Roberts Moore lived in Fairbanks for a number of years, giving birth to a daughter in 1909, practicing law, and entering the society pages of the newspaper with reports of her parties and card games. By 1917, she and her family had moved to Tacoma, where her husband continued to practice dentistry, though it is less clear whether Roberts Moore continued the practice of law. She died in 1950.

Isabel Ambler Gilman: Educator, Lawyer, and Author

Born in Yorkshire, England, around 1864, Isabel Ambler Gilman was educated in England and Wales and traveled to the United States in 1888, where she worked as an educator, writer, and lawyer, according to Juneau historian R. N. De Armond. After studying law and graduating from the Lincoln-Jefferson University, Gilman became a member of the bar at Olympia, Washington, in 1909. A year later, while living in southeast Alaska, she gained admittance to the Alaska Bar, according to De Armond. This would make her, as of this counting, the second woman to be admitted to practice law.

Gilman wrote extensively about her experiences in Alaska and her work as a school principal and teacher in Petersburg, Kanakanak, Seldovia, and Rampart. It is also noted in biographical material in her articles that she practiced law in Seldovia.

According to De Armond, while Gilman was in Petersburg she "won a significant victory for the fishermen of southeastern Alaska when she proved to the satisfaction of the Washington State Commissioner of Fisheries that the Dolly Varden is a char, not a trout, and hence could legally be marketed in that state."

Gilman moved to New York in 1920, where she continued to write and publish. She died in 1949.

Dr. Aline Chenot Baskerville Bradley Beegler: Singer, Doctor and Lawyer

Fairbanks was home to both the first and third women to become members of the Alaska bar. Dr. Aline Chenot Baskerville Bradley Beegler had been living in Fairbanks for more than a decade when she was admitted to the Alaska bar in 1920. Like Mildred Hermann, Beegler would acquire her legal education and license to practice while advocating change.

Born in Paris, France, in 1867, Aline Chenot trained first to be a professional singer. In 1886, she left Europe with her family and moved to the United States. Eight years later, at twenty-seven years old, she married Dr. Thomas Hardy Baskerville, who had a medical practice in Pennsylvania. Perhaps inspired by her husband, Aline turned her energy toward becoming a physician. Undeterred by limited medical education options open to women at the turn of the century, she entered the Woman's Medical College of Pennsylvania and graduated in 1903. Aline and her husband relocated to a small town northwest of Pittsburgh, where Aline obtained a license to practice. There, she spent a couple of years in medical practice, mainly doing physical examinations for the Lady Maccabees, a women's organization affiliated with the fraternal Knights of the Maccabees that provided relief for destitute families.

In the summer of 1907, the doctors Baskerville traveled to Fairbanks, Alaska, where they hoped the cool, dry air would alleviate Thomas Baskerville's asthma. Aline began to sing with local music groups and in church, where she became the choir director. When she and her husband opened up their medical practice, Aline became the second female doctor in the territory.

A year later, Aline cared for her husband as he suffered from an inoperable tumor. Thomas Baskerville died September 8, 1908. Within a few months, Aline married James Freeman Bradley, a "tall, handsome Canadian miner." Bradley had guided Aline and her husband on a hunt and had fallen in love with Aline.

In her early forties, Aline continued to practice medicine and continued to take an active interest in Fairbanks' social and civic affairs. When the consolidated Fairbanks Banking Company/Washington-Alaska Bank failed unexpectedly in 1911, Aline joined a committee of angry depositors to investigate. The focus of the investigation was wrongdoing by E. T. Barnette, founder of Fairbanks and one of the bank's directors. A grand jury failed to indict Barnette on mismanagement and fraud, leaving a bitter taste in the mouths of depositors who felt that their money had been stolen.

Aline organized a group of women to protest the grand jury's failure to indict and the corruption of bank officials. She investigated those serving on the grand jury and found that many had close relationships with either the bank, Barnette, or Barnette's lawyers. Aline, along with other depositors, petitioned the governor as well as the district court to take action.

Barnette was finally charged and arrested. Although Barnette was indicted on eleven counts, including embezzlement, making false reports, and perjury, he was convicted of only one misdemeanor and fined $1,000.

The result angered Aline and the other women on her committee. They organized a "burning in effigy" of the bank's attorneys, John McGinn and John Clark, along with a third figure labeled "Justice." More than one hundred people turned out to watch the burning on the frozen Chena River in January 1913.

Three months later, with the convening of the first territorial legislature, a Territorial Banking Act was passed to bring all Alaska banks under governmental regulation.

The Barnette banking scandal provided Aline with a strong example of how much power attorneys wielded. She continued to use her medical training to advocate for public policy issues that would benefit the health and welfare of Alaskans, but she must have considered how much more she could accomplish with a better understanding of the law and even a license to practice.

Elected Fairbanks city physician in 1913, Aline pushed for improved ventilation in the schools, greater medical care for indigents, and inspection of milk products. Appointed by Governor J. F. A. Strong to the Territorial Board of Medical Examiners, she began to correspond with Judge James Wickersham and get more deeply involved in political issues, including prohibition and school funding. Simultaneously, she began to study law with Wickersham's law partner, Fairbanks lawyer Albert R. Heilig. Like Hermann, she understood the advantages of knowing the law when garnering support for change.

In 1917, Congress passed the Bone Dry Law extending prohibition to Alaska, capping Aline's temperance efforts. That year she also passed the bar exam. Among the examiners was lawyer John Clark, whom she had burned in effigy just four years earlier for his role in the Barnette case. The committee recommended she be admitted to the Alaska bar.

Citizenship questions, though, prevented her from being admitted immediately. With the death of her Canadian husband in 1918, and her subsequent marriage to Michael Beegler, a miner from Livengood and naturalized citizen, in 1919, these questions resolved. In 1920, at fifty-three years old, Dr. Aline Chenot Baskerville Bradley Beegler became the third woman to be admitted to practice law in Alaska.

She continued to practice medicine and also practiced law. Although she and her husband started to spend winters in warmer climates, in the fall of 1922, the city council of Livengood appointed her city magistrate and legal advisor and paid her $50 a month. In 1930, the Beeglers sold their Fairbanks home and moved to California. Dr. Aline Beegler died in 1947 at the age of seventy-five.

The community of Fairbanks, located in the interior, was more isolated than Juneau and Nome, and may have provided fewer barriers and more opportunities for women lawyers, at least in the case of Natalie Roberts Moore and Beegler. Although the independent-minded nature of these two women certainly contributed.

Roberts, the first woman admitted to the Alaska bar, studied law at a time when very few women turned to law as a profession. That she had already become chief clerk in the legal department of the Northern Pacific Railway before traveling to Fairbanks indicated an ambition and adventuresome spirit. As a single female lawyer she gained employment in Fairbanks law offices and eventually began her own practice after marrying. That she continued to practice law while her husband practiced dentistry, especially at a time when many women stopped working outside the home when married, demonstrated her independence and satisfaction in her chosen profession.

Dr. Aline Beegler was a woman of multiple talents and intellect, which she put toward improving the social and economic welfare of her community. Adept at the arts, sciences, and the law, she was a Renaissance woman never afraid to jump into a complex situation. Although she came to the law later in life, it flowed naturally from all that she had accomplished to that point. Acquiring legal education, passing the bar exam, being admitted to practice, and practicing law, in her fifties, reflected a lifetime devoted to acquiring education and skills to remain engaged and effective in her community.

When Mildred Hermann became a practicing member of the Alaska bar in 1935, she had a husband and two children. She didn't turn to the law to climb out of the Depression and support her family. She was not dissuaded by the social norms of the day, which frowned upon a woman working when her husband had a job. Mildred Hermann embraced the law because she wanted more influence, especially when it came to Alaska's fight for statehood. She turned to the law to have the prestige and standing of being a lawyer, the ability to provide legal analysis of issues, and to be an effective advocate for the people and causes she believed in.

It's difficult to compare the opportunities afforded each of these first female lawyers in Alaska with opportunities they might have had outside. What is true, is that like men who came to practice in Alaska, they made their own opportunities, and the communities in which they chose to live contributed to their success.

Although Hermann was not the first woman to practice law in Alaska, she's often been called this. It is likely because of the time she practiced, the changes occurring in Alaska, and the lasting impact that she made as a female lawyer.

Hermann: Nome's Favorite Lawyer

Haaland remembered a story Hermann told her about Nome in the mid-1940s. Hermann had a client in Nome at the time who needed some work done that required her to travel there. She let her client know when she'd be coming. Normally, Nome had a judge, a US attorney, and a lawyer in private practice, but within a few weeks all three were gone. The judge left town, the US attorney was fired, and the lawyer died in a drowning accident.

When Hermann arrived, the plane terminal was filled with people who'd heard a lawyer was coming to town. They all wanted to talk with her. Instead of staying a day or two to deal with her client, Hermann stayed six weeks. "All she did was talk to people and find out what they wanted, whether it was a will or a deed or whatever."

Hermann enjoyed the practice of law, especially criminal cases, even though they were not as well-paying as other cases. Alaska Natives made up a disproportionate number of defendants in criminal cases, and Hermann came to the belief that there was little justice in trying Natives by "white man's law." She had no solution that could address the fact that the Native and white points of view were "diametrically opposed."

She told the story of one of her Alaska Native clients who had been charged with murder. She was quite proud of the fact that she had gotten the charge reduced to manslaughter and a lenient sentence. He was sent to the federal penitentiary at McNeil Island in Washington's Puget Sound to serve his sentence, since there were no federal jails in Alaska. A few weeks after arriving at prison, she received a letter from her client:

"It is just grand down here," he wrote. "We have free movies twice a week, baseball games every Saturday, a fine library where we can read and study, and a night school where you can learn anything you want to. I play in the prison band, I have fine food to eat, a nice room and a good bed, I can have a bath whenever I want it, too and I shall really be sorry when my term is up and I have to go back to the village and live as I used to."

Hermann forecast that when her client was released and went back to his "lonely little village where he had lived in poverty and squalor most of his life, he will spend his time telling the boys all about it. I wager there will be a crime wave in that village such as it has never known before. But I won't be getting any new client there. My reputation for getting them off with light sentences is too firmly established."

The measures of success, the judgment of conditions and lifestyles that Hermann writes of, are those of a territorial lawyer who more than most would be sympathetic to clients with little power. Hermann's assessment provides insight into the historic inadequacies and inequities of Alaska's territorial legal system.

Haaland: Answering the Phone at 2 AM

At the end of the war and with the folding of the Office of Price Administration, Hermann remained in Juneau. She devoted more time to her private practice, working with civic organizations and the Statehood Committee. Haaland then traveled to Cordova for a job as US commissioner.

An isolated community of a thousand people near the mouth of the Copper River, Cordova had one airport built during the war and a port on the southeastern end of Prince William Sound. Historic home to seasonal residents, Athabascan and Tlingit Natives known as Eyak, Cordova had been an important shipping port for copper, silver, and gold before Haaland arrived. The Copper River and Northwest Railroad carried over $200 million worth of precious metals from the Bonanza-Kennecott Mines to Cordova between 1911 and 1938, when the mine closed. By 1945 fishing had become Cordova's main industry.

As commissioner, Haaland's duties included those today associated with several positions: justice of the peace, coroner, probate judge, recorder. Her pay consisted of fees rather than a salary. Some fees were collected on the spot, but other fees required a tedious written report to the federal government. Only then, after filing the report, would Haaland receive $10 for a misdemeanor or arraignment in her court. Walter Hodge, the only other attorney in Cordova, offered Haaland work in his office to supplement her commissioner pay.

"In small towns where people didn't know who to go to for help, they figured they'd start with the commissioner," Haaland said. "The phone would ring at two o'clock in the morning . . . sometimes drunks who didn't know who else to call. But it was a fascinating job," she recalled.

"I remember very well the first time I was called out as coroner. . . . I had never even seen a dead person before. It was an old Native, one of the oldest in the [Eyak] village. . . . It was a natural death but it was still an experience. He had been dead for some time."

Haaland remembered another case in which a woman was brought before her for public drunkenness. "She said she'd like to explain what had happened. She was very serious. I said, 'All right, what happened?' She said, 'I went to the doctor and he gave me some medicine and he warned me that it wasn't a good idea to drink while I was taking that medicine,' she said. 'I tried it. And he was right. I just shouldn't have been drinking while I was taking that medicine. Boy, I sure learned my lesson. I'll never take any more medicine.'

"She was so serious," Haaland laughed.

After eighteen months in Cordova, in 1948 Haaland moved to Anchorage to clerk for Anthony Dimond, federal judge for the Third Division. Haaland, Dimond's first law clerk, listened to the judge in court and helped research the law.

"He was a fine man, one of the finest people I've ever met and a very good lawyer. He never went to law school either. He came up here to look for gold and then he studied law in [Tom Donohoe's] office."

Women Commissioners: Nora Guinn

Haaland's job as commissioner did not require a law license but did require a good amount of common sense. Women often served as commissioner, a federal posting, and magistrate, a similar position on the local level. Commissioners and magistrates were available to their communities on a regular basis. This was especially important in Alaska where three or four federal district court judges served the entire territory. Although judges traveled in their districts, they spent most of their time in Juneau, Fairbanks, Nome, and Anchorage.

Nora Guinn, the first Alaska Native to be appointed district court judge in Alaska, served as US commissioner, deputy magistrate, and district court magistrate in Bethel from 1959 to 1967 before being appointed judge. Born in Akiak in 1920, she went to boarding school in Eklutna and high school in Portland, Oregon. Before becoming commissioner, Guinn taught with the Bureau of Indian Affairs in Tununak.

Guinn's reputation as a fair and impartial jurist came from her knowledge of the community as well as her ability to conduct hearings in Yupik, so that those in her court clearly understood the charges and reasons for her decisions. After her retirement she was awarded an honorary doctorate from the University of Alaska.

Hermann and Haaland Help Draft Alaska's Constitution

In 1955 a notice went out in the newspapers across Alaska encouraging citizens to run for a seat at Alaska's Constitutional Convention. For years a group of Alaskans had been appealing to the federal government to give the territory statehood status and the ability to govern itself. Stumbling blocks included a fear that the territory did not have the resources necessary to support itself as a state and strong outside business interests that did not want the state to regulate and tax their operations. It was decided that a Constitutional Convention would be held to develop the framework for laws for Alaska and to demonstrate the territory's readiness for statehood.

Hermann had already been testifying in Washington, DC, in favor of statehood, and lobbying. In 1950, she spoke at a Senate hearing and dispelled the notion that Alaska couldn't afford statehood: "If we cannot buy steak, we will eat beans. We will fit the pattern to the cloth. If we cannot make the kind of dress we want, we will make one that will cover us anyway, and we are perfectly willing to pull in our belts and do without some things for the purpose of statehood."

Haaland had been less involved in the statehood movement, but when the opportunity arose to help draft a state constitution, the laws that would govern the legal practice of the future state, she couldn't pass it up. "It was the chance of a lifetime and I just had to try it," Haaland said of running for a delegate seat. "Even if I failed, at least I'd know that I'd tried. It was my first entry into politics. I just squeaked in."

Hermann never doubted that she would become a delegate and reserved her hotel room in Fairbanks even before election results had been counted.

Dorothy Awes Haaland signing the Alaska Constitution at the end of the Constitutional Convention. Courtesy Roger Haaland.

Haaland and Hermann were two out of six women elected to the convention. As lawyers, they were in good company since eleven of the male delegates were also lawyers.

Although both Haaland and Hermann fiercely defended the rights of women to enjoy all the same benefits as men, their approach to securing this equality differed. Hermann, like many at the convention, felt that women were equal under the law and that it was unnecessary to enunciate the right in the constitution. Active in national groups, including the National Association of Women Lawyers, National Association of Press Women, Soroptimist Club, Republican Women, and Federation of Women, Hermann could easily compare the opportunities she'd been afforded in Alaska to those of women outside. Alaska already treated its women well, she'd benefited greatly, and saw no need for Alaska's constitution to add any special protections and support. Haaland disagreed, but it would take until long after the Constitutional Convention for her feminist view to finally prevail.

After the Constitutional Convention ended, Haaland married Ragnar Haaland. But her first entry into politics left her with a desire to try again. She ran and won a seat in the last territorial legislature, which met between 1957 and 1959. She spent the two sixty-day sessions in Juneau staying with Hermann and renewing that friendship. By the end of the 1959 session, Alaska was the forty-ninth state and Haaland, eight months pregnant with her first child, retired from politics.

Haaland: The Last Word

Although retired from elected politics, Haaland was far from retired. In 1960, she went to work in the attorney general's office in Anchorage. Unlike today, the office handled both civil cases and criminal cases— the latter are now given to the district attorney's office. Haaland, who became chief of the office, did not enjoy the criminal cases. Always drawn to work on behalf of women, she helped with child support collection and developed an admiration for the capacity of women "to survive without knowing if they had a job or a meal."

By the 1960s, Haaland had been joined by a handful of women in the practice of law, though no woman had been appointed to the state court bench. Few women challenged the inequities women faced in Alaska and the rest of the country. "I have been a feminist as long as I can remember," Haaland said. "It was a really lonely world out there because one would almost feel as if there was something wrong with me. Other women don't seem to be bothered by these things. And you're reluctant to talk about it. You do feel lonely. You always wonder. So, when the feminist movement broke out in the late 1960s and all these people came out of the closet, so to speak, I found I wasn't alone in the world."

Haaland helped found the Anchorage Women's Liberation Society and, in 1972, Alaska became one of the first states to ratify the Equal Rights Amendment. A year later Alaskans incorporated the Equal Rights Amendment into the Alaska state constitution.

Haaland's efforts would contribute to the word "sex" becoming part Alaska's constitution, providing "no person is to be denied the enjoyment of any civil or political right because of sex, race, color, creed, or national origin."

Generational Divide

Although divided by a generation, Haaland and Hermann used their education and status as lawyers to promote change and engage fully in professional and civic life. Hermann, center stage in Alaska and nationally, would contribute greatly to Alaska's statehood movement. Her arguments were instructive and colorful.

Haaland came to the law and Alaska to fulfill a passion to do things her way and to live a life less constrained by the societal conventions of what a woman should or should not do. Both women pushed the envelope as far as it would go in their time. Haaland would apply for a judgeship twice and be refused. The first woman to be appointed judge would be Dorothy Tyner in 1968, the first woman to be on the Alaska Superior Court would be Karen Hunt in 1983, the first woman to be on the Alaska Court of Appeals would be Marjorie Allard in 2012, and the first woman to be on Alaska's Supreme Court would be Dana Fabe in 1996. Morgan Christen became the first woman appointed to the Ninth Circuit Court of Appeals from Alaska in 2012.

The Equal Rights Amendment has not yet been added to the US Constitution.

John Hellenthal. Anchorage Bar Association Oral History of Territorial Lawyers, Pamela Cravez. Joint archives of the Alaska Court System and the Alaska Bar Association.

7 ★

Hellenthal Chooses Anchorage

Opinionated, blunt, and eager to talk about the characters he knew so well in the territorial bar, John Hellenthal sat in his Anchorage law office on a Saturday in the spring of 1982 wearing a T-shirt; his white hair was long and his face flushed. Reminders of the past surrounded him. A scrapbook of Juneau newspaper clippings from the early 1900s sat on his desk. A photo of his father, Third Division District Court Judge Simon Hellenthal, hung on the wall next to a photo of the president who appointed him judge, Franklin D. Roosevelt. And, though it no longer housed the federal district court, the stately white federal courthouse where Simon Hellenthal presided in the 1940s was just across the street.

It had been forty years since John moved from his hometown of Juneau to Anchorage. In his late sixties, Hellenthal evinced the youthful enthusiasm of a prodigal son, with the privilege of being born into an Alaskan legal dynasty and the freedom to define his own progressive politics and legal practice.

Statehood advocate, Constitutional Convention delegate, territorial legislator, pugilistic trial lawyer, and counsel for Anchorage's underclass—these positions were all John Hellenthal's legacy. Although both his father and uncle were long dead, a "Hellenthal and Hellenthal" sign faced out from his window onto Fourth Avenue.

John Hellenthal's father, Simon, and his uncle, Jack Hellenthal, both lawyers, came to Juneau early in the town's history. Jack arrived in

1900 from Wyoming and represented first, the Treadwell gold mine and later, with his brother Simon, the Alaska Juneau Mine. Serving as counsel to the largest businesses in town gave the Hellenthals entrée into Juneau's highest social circles. But John Hellenthal remembers his family's unease within the small town's growing aristocracy.

"My father and uncle were Dutchmen, they were fiercely independent people and they didn't have any use for . . . the way Juneau was, a bunch of ancestor-worshippers," Hellenthal said.

Many of Hellenthal's maternal relatives had mined in Coeur d'Alene, British Columbia, and Alaska. The precocious Hellenthal vacillated between a fascination for his family's legal practice and the physical challenge of mining.

Born in 1915, Hellenthal's pride in family background took root when, as a child, he helped out in the family law office. The office was in an impressive three-story building with the Hellenthal name emblazoned on the front; it also housed a theater and bank. The law offices, which Hellenthal visited after school each day, took up the entire third floor.

"My uncle knew an Indian Chief by the name of Anacohosh," Hellenthal said. "He had quite a few dealings with Anacohosh." Anacohosh spent so much time in the waiting room that he became a fixture. "My uncle bought him a Civil War uniform and he used to wear this uniform and sit there, straight as a poker," remembered Hellenthal.

Hellenthal tells this story to demonstrate his family's refusal to support practices of racial discrimination and segregation that were prevalent in Juneau at the time. It is interesting that even in the telling of this story to show sensitivity, the depth of discrimination shines through. Discrimination in Alaska against Alaska Natives (few African Americans lived in Juneau until during and after World War II) was pervasive. Natives were often barred from voting in elections, forced to sit separately in movie theaters, required to use separate entrances to grocery stores, barred from joining certain churches, kept from living in certain areas of town, and faced huge discrimination in other aspects of conventional life. No Alaska Natives attended Hellenthal's elementary and high schools.

Hellenthal pointed out that perennial school board member R. E. Robertson was a strong supporter of segregation. This kind of closed mindedness typified for Hellenthal the "big time" lawyers in Juneau.

According to Hellenthal, the Faulkner Banfield and Robertson Monagle firms jealously guarded their monopoly on Juneau's legal

The courthouse in Valdez served south central Alaska until it burned down in 1940. UAF-1975-0043-00019.

business. "They didn't want any competition and they discouraged it by running the competition out of town, calling them radicals. . . . Juneau was always a closed shop," Hellenthal said.

Although encouraged to enter the legal profession, Hellenthal harbored dreams of mining. He spent summers home from college working for the Alaska Juneau Mine. Starting above ground, in the mill, Hellenthal soon got his wish to go underground. There he sweated and toiled with foreign-born workers hired for the least desirable mining jobs.

Although he enjoyed the physical labor of mining, Hellenthal began to realize he might be able to do more to help his fellow workers by practicing law. He could practice for the common good, as pure economic gain left a distaste for him.

Still, what he saw of the Juneau practice held little appeal. Which is probably why when he met successful lawyers who practiced outside of Juneau, he was fascinated. Lawyers from Nome, Fairbanks, Cordova, Seward, and Valdez traveled to Juneau for sessions of the territorial legislature and stopped on their way to and from Seattle by steamship. Many visited the Hellenthal home where conversations naturally turned to the law, lawyers, and judges.

Hellenthal spoke with admiration of two of these lawyers whom he found particularly interesting. These were the kind of lawyers that caused him to think that practicing law might not be so bad.

Warren Taylor: Crude but Juries Loved Him

Judge Simon Hellenthal used to tell his son that he'd never seen a prosecutor who could appeal to a Cordova jury better than Warren Taylor. Taylor was the district attorney for Cordova while Simon Hellenthal presided as judge there.

"Warren was crude," Judge Hellenthal told his son. "He didn't put on any show of erudition, but he could talk to a jury in language that they understood and they loved him. He got so many convictions that everybody was happy when he decided to become a private lawyer."

Taylor knew the community well, arriving as an eighteen-year-old in 1909 and signing on with the Copper River and Northwestern Railroad. He worked his way up to fireman and locomotive engineer, carrying copper and other precious metals from the Bonanza-Kennecott Mines to Cordova's port on Prince William Sound. After World War I, Taylor studied law in an office and entered the bar.

Taylor not only appealed to jurors, he also appealed to voters and was elected to the territorial legislature in 1933 for the first of many times, making Juneau a regular stop for him. Taylor eventually settled in Fairbanks, served at Alaska's Constitutional Convention in 1955, and took an active role in fashioning Alaska's formal bar association and state judiciary. After statehood, he would run unsuccessfully for governor and in 1965 was appointed Superior Court judge in Fairbanks.

John McGinn: Prospecting and Practicing Law from Nome to Fairbanks

Hellenthal's greatest admiration, though, was reserved for John McGinn. Another Fairbanks attorney, McGinn's career dated back to the Nome gold rush. A diminutive Irishman, McGinn owned several gold mines, working them himself, and practiced mining law. One of Alaska's more formally trained lawyers, McGinn graduated with a law degree from the University of Oregon and practiced with his brother, Henry, in the 1890s. Although his brother had been a US senator from Oregon and would later serve as judge in the Fourth Judicial District in Oregon, McGinn left the relative security of family practice and connections for the excitement and adventure of Alaska.

Like thousands of others, McGinn arrived in Nome the summer of 1900 in search of gold. While Judge Arthur Noyes was busy helping Alexander McKenzie loot claims, the twenty-nine-year-old McGinn was prospecting on nearby Saturday Creek. As efforts were made to clean up Judge Noyes' administration, McGinn was appointed assistant US district attorney in the fall of 1900 and less than a year later US attorney.

McGinn followed the mining trails throughout the territory and into Canada, prospecting and representing mine owners and earning a reputation as one of Alaska's best mining lawyers. In 1905 following the Interior gold rush, he settled in Fairbanks (where he helped successfully defend E. T. Barnette in the bank failure case and was subsequently burned in effigy by Dr. Aline Beegler) and continued to travel extensively pursuing mining ventures up and down the West Coast.

Hellenthal remembered McGinn, in later years, spending the summers in Fairbanks and the winters in California.

McGinn, Taylor, and other territorial lawyers traveling through Juneau contrasted sharply with the successful Juneau practitioners who were steadily becoming more like their conservative lower forty-eight colleagues. Outside of Juneau, lawyers still embraced the independent spirit and unconventional lifestyles of other Alaskans. So did John Hellenthal.

George Grigsby: Foxy, But Totally Undependable

As much as Hellenthal craved breaking free from Juneau's staid and stratified legal community, he wasn't prepared to embrace all of Alaska's esteemed gold rush lawyers. He found little to admire about George Grigsby.

Grigsby was a drunk, Hellenthal said, adding that "he was foxy: he had a good sense of humor, a quick wit but he was totally undependable. He'd never show up in court."

The sight of an aging Grigsby sleeping off benders in the Juneau court cloakroom made a lasting impression on the teenage John Hellenthal. Although Hellenthal admits Grigsby had seen better days, to him Grigsby was first a "drunk."

Many of Alaska's early lawyers, especially trial lawyers, social in nature and eager to share war stories, often got caught in the vortex of liquor. Colleagues became accustomed to making allowances and frequently marveled at an attorney's uncanny ability to switch from notorious drunk to brilliant attorney.

Even Norman Banfield more kindly assessed Grigsby's legal talents than Hellenthal. But Banfield probably never faced Grigsby in court and certainly did not deal with him in the political arena. Banfield merely observed Grigsby from a careful distance.

When John Hellenthal moved to Anchorage in the 1940s to practice law, he found the Anchorage lawyers, many of them new to the territory, had elevated George Grigsby to superstardom, making him president of the Anchorage Bar Association for life and celebrating Grigsby as the best trial lawyer in Alaska.

"I Hate to See You Go Up There, John"

Even before attending law school, Hellenthal had decided to move to Anchorage. He had no interest in being one of the kids who "stayed in Juneau [and] drank themselves to death . . . waiting for their parents to die so they could inherit whatever they had."

The first time he saw Anchorage, in 1932, it was a "dirty damn place," Hellenthal remembered. Established in 1915 to support the building of the Alaska Railroad, the small town of about 3,000 people had only a few unpaved dusty streets in the 1930s and none of the gold rush history, business, or territorial government ties of Juneau. To the young Hellenthal, who shared Anchorage's birth year, the town offered an opportunity for him to make his own mark.

Referred to as the longest bar in Alaska for the number of drinking establishments per block, Anchorage felt like the "wild west."

There was only one hitch to Hellenthal's plan to make Anchorage his home. When he graduated from Notre Dame's law school in 1939, his father, Simon, was the district court judge for the Third Judicial Division, which included Anchorage. When President Roosevelt appointed Simon Hellenthal judge in 1934, the courthouse had been located in Valdez. But in 1940, the Valdez courthouse burned down and Judge Hellenthal moved his court to Anchorage.

John Hellenthal put off moving, since practicing law in front of his father, the judge, would be awkward. Instead, he joined his Uncle Jack's legal practice in Juneau. But he wasn't happy about it. In the summer of 1941, with the war escalating in Europe, Hellenthal enlisted. While waiting to be inducted, he traveled to Anchorage, not to practice law, but to work as a carpenter.

Anchorage Transformed by World War II

Greater than any gold rush to hit Alaska, the military buildup in Anchorage in response to World War II swept away traces of the small town that Hellenthal had seen in 1932.

With Hitler's invasion of Belgium and the Netherlands in May 1940, the federal government finally acted on Major General William "Billy" Mitchell's observation in 1935 that Alaska "is the most important strategic place in the world." Because of Alaska's proximity to three continents via air, Congress appropriated funds for construction of a permanent airbase in Anchorage: Fort Richardson. By the time Paris fell to the Germans on June 14, 1940, construction was underway on what would amount to a city just four miles northeast of downtown Anchorage.

Fort Richardson (in the twenty-first century, Joint Base Elmendorf-Richardson or "JBER") would have housing for more than 8,000 military personnel—double Anchorage's prewar population—a hospital, two runways, multiple hangars, water, power, and fuel.

Everything from concrete for the runways to fuel for the planes would be shipped into the territory. Between 1941 and 1945 the federal government spent more than $1 billion on its military presence in Alaska, transforming the territory forever. Alaska's total population in 1939 was a little more than 72,000 people; in 1948 there were an additional 152,000 military personnel in Alaska. Airfields to accommodate military aircraft were built throughout the state, including Fairbanks, Juneau, and all along the Aleutian chain. In 1942, the lend-lease program began routing US aircraft through Alaska and Siberia to the Russian front with Germany.

In November 1942, the Alaska Highway connecting the territory with the contiguous lower forty-eight states opened. Until that time all people and freight arrived in Alaska by ship or plane. With the work of 11,500 army troops, 40 percent of whom were African American, along with 6,000 civilian workers, the 1,420-mile road was constructed in nine months.

Suddenly, Alaska, which had receded further and further from public and political consciousness since the gold rush, became a place of strategic importance.

In the summer of 1941 more than 3,000 civilian construction workers were hired to build housing and infrastructure to accommodate the military presence in Anchorage. Among them was twenty-six-year-old John Hellenthal.

"I liked working with my hands, so I said, 'I'll go to Anchorage and get a job as a carpenter,' didn't know anything about it, I couldn't even drive a nail," Hellenthal said. He had finally found that Alaskan frontier where anything was possible.

Hellenthal promptly set to work amid all the others, toiling around the clock during the long-lit hours of the summer. Although housing and food shortages plagued the city, the economy boomed.

In Juneau, Hellenthal had earned $3.60 a day working underground in the mines. In Anchorage he could make $12 a day as a carpenter.

"Those people up there don't know the value of money," friends in Juneau had warned Hellenthal. "They'd treat a ten dollar bill like it was a dollar bill."

Hellenthal admitted it was "a hell of a big difference in pay," but added that he never trusted what people in Juneau told him about Anchorage. They were always telling him that they hated to see him go, predicting that the "bubble would burst."

By the time the army inducted Hellenthal in September 1941, he'd become a "fair carpenter," and more determined than ever to make his future in Anchorage.

Anchorage Lawyers in the 1940s

In 1945, with the end of the war and his father replaced on the bench by Anthony Dimond, John Hellenthal slipped easily into the diverse group of lawyers practicing in Anchorage.

Although the military presence had declined dramatically, Anchorage's civilian population had doubled. During the 1940s, Anchorage would overtake Juneau and southeast Alaska and continue to grow, defying those in Juneau who had cautioned Hellenthal. Anchorage's bubble would not burst.

The dozen or so men practicing law perpetuated a frontier-style informality. Some, including Judge Dimond, had never been to law school, instead apprenticing in a law office. The judge furthered the informality by never wearing a robe on the bench.

Although backgrounds differed, attorneys handled mostly criminal work, divorces, personal injury cases, bankruptcies, contracts, land issues, and applications for citizenship. Anchorage business was that of

any small town of 10,000: insurance, banking, small commercial interests, and some mining. Nothing like the salmon, gold, and steamship
business in the southeast.

Left to Right: Stan McCutcheon, J. L. McCarrey, Harold Butcher, John Manders,
Dorothy Tyner, Karl Drager, J. Gerald Williams, Edward V. Davis, and George
Grigsby. Joint archives of the Alaska Court System and the Alaska Bar Association.

Dorothy Tyner and the Anchorage Bar

In 1945, Dorothy Tyner traveled to Anchorage to see what prospects
might be like for practicing law. The Anchorage bar wined and
dined the young female attorney. Tyner became the first woman to
practice in Anchorage. She would also become one of Alaska's first
female judges after statehood.

Because of this, there was little to cause any great divisions among
lawyers. Any professional adversarial relationships were easily tem-
pered by a shared bottle of "Old Grand Dad," a good practical joke, or a
long weekend of duck hunting.

Where court rules and codes of conduct today define legal practice, in
the 1940s Anchorage lawyers depended upon a more personal approach.
A phone call, a handshake, or a simple exchange of words often sufficed

in legal transactions. Attorneys knew each other well enough to know how long it might take for one to get an agreement reduced to writing, or if another was going to have a hangover the next day in court. A contract between two parties did not need to be complicated by two attorneys when one would do.

Anchorage juries exhibited an independence of spirit, their verdicts relying more on a lawyer's dramatic performance and appeal to pragmatism than on the letter of the law.

And, if by chance, a lawyer found himself being the one charged with a crime, he could rely on his brethren to come to his aid.

Lawyer Indicted for "Being a Pimp"

In 1942, assistant US attorney Noel Wennblom brought a case against attorney Karl Drager, charging him with being a pimp and keeping a bawdy house. The case came before the court on a Friday and was tossed out for lack of evidence by Saturday. Grigsby, Warren Cuddy (also president of the First National Bank of Anchorage), and Tom Donohoe (law partner to Anthony Dimond) were among the lawyers who represented Drager.

The case is buried in an old court journal with handwritten entries of charges brought during the war years. The journal is riddled with cases against prostitutes and bawdy houses with names like Nugget Rooms and Globe Rooms. Nearly every Anchorage attorney is listed as representing these clients at one time or another, though Drager and Grigsby represented them most frequently. The case is not among stories that have survived by being told and retold by territorial lawyers.

According to the journal entries, the Monday after the judge dismissed the case, Grigsby and Drager were back in court winning trials for their clients.

The hierarchical nature of Juneau's bar was not so evident in Anchorage. Attorneys took cases that came their way. Even as firms began to grow in Anchorage, it would remain far different from what Hellenthal had experienced in Juneau.

The Floating Court

One of Hellenthal's fondest recollections of practicing law during territorial years in the Third Division was participating in the floating court.

Every two years, in the spring, the Third Division judge packed up his law books and took a coast guard cutter from Seward to Kodiak and then all along the Aleutian chain to hold court. The US attorney or one of his assistants and private defense attorneys went along, providing a "full-service" court, since it was rare to find an attorney in any of the communities. On occasion a doctor, a dentist, and others accompanied the judge to further serve people far from Alaska's population centers. These communities presented the court with all kinds of problems, but mainly people sought naturalization and divorce services.

Hellenthal, who participated in floating court sessions, remembers, "They used to grant divorces in school houses, cabins. They held court in the weirdest places, any place that had a roof."

In Alaska's small coastal towns—like Dutch Harbor, Atka, Adak, Unga, Simak, Anchetkov, and Naknek—the spring arrival of court, after a long dark winter and many months without legal services, became cause for celebrations. The court provided theater to residents of these small, isolated communities.

Hellenthal remembered cannery workers in Naknek filling the room when trials began. They'd take the day as a holiday, have a few drinks, and come to watch the lawyers and judge from Anchorage. People lined up to present lawyers with their patchwork legal documents and have them repaired to more permanent and valid legal states. Thus the lawyers replaced marriage certificates issued by the postmaster and validated with cigar coupons with more legally binding papers.

Trial work and the floating court provided many opportunities for socializing and excitement. But as a young man with greater ambition, Hellenthal decided to take a job in the Davis and Renfrew firm, one of the few that had more work than two partners could manage on their own.

Davis and Renfrew: Bill Collecting to Banking Law

Outgoing and gregarious, William "Bill" Renfrew grew up in Idaho, the son of a wealthy banker. Rebellious by nature, Renfrew lost his father's backing when he refused to go directly to college and instead first worked as a used car salesman. Renfrew worked his way through the University of Idaho Law School, where he met Edward Davis.

Davis—quiet, smart, and detail-oriented—was drawn to Renfrew's spirited enthusiasm. When the two arrived in Anchorage in 1939 with their families, they rented a small office from Z. J. Loussac in the Loussac-Sogn building. Bill collecting sustained the firm until the military arrived in 1941.

"The Army Will Pay Me ... You Won't"

With the arrival of troops came the need for housing and land. Few provisions had been made; land had not even been cleared for tents. With an expertise in land title work gained in Idaho, Davis and Renfrew offered their services to the military's land acquisition officer.

People who owned property in the area north of downtown were given twenty-four-hour notice to vacate. Davis and Renfrew researched the land titles, and Renfrew, who knew many of the landowners, went around with the army colonel negotiating settlement terms, according to Mary Fasnacht. Fasnacht, interviewed in the 1980s, worked with Renfrew and later became his wife.

To those who complained to Renfrew that he should be representing his friends, not the army, he responded, "The Army will pay me and you won't," remembered Fasnacht.

With the new long runway on the military base, air traffic increased and the population grew so rapidly that grocery shelves were always empty. Finally, housing got so tight that the military ordered the families of people doing work for the army to leave. Renfrew's and Davis' families were ordered to leave Alaska because the two men had a contract with the army to do the title work. Their secretary, Fasnacht, however, managed to avoid the arm of the military since the army did not have a contract with her.

Renfrew and Fasnacht traveled throughout Alaska—Wrangel, Ketchikan, Juneau, Whitehorse, Fairbanks, Bethel—doing the army's title work. Renfrew, at the government's behest, even took a British ship out to the Aleutians. Fasnacht did most of the paperwork for the quiet title actions, the kind of task she had done back in Idaho. That left Renfrew and Davis free to handle other legal business generated from the war effort and the Anchorage boom. By the end of the war, the Davis and Renfrew firm was the most successful in Anchorage and was well known outside of the city as well.

Hunting and Banking

Elmer Rasmuson, who in 1943 began to help his father run Alaska's largest bank, the National Bank of Alaska (NBA), wrote in his memoirs that he "learned a lot from Bill [Renfrew] about hunting, fishing and flying."

Renfrew and Rasmuson, born the same year, 1909, became close friends, and Rasmuson came to appreciate Renfrew's "colorful character and picturesque manner of speech." The Renfrew, Davis, and Rasmuson families shared hunting and fishing trips, cabins on lakes, and flying adventures. Rasmuson also turned to the firm for personal and banking legal business.

Davis served as Anchorage counsel in the formation of the Rasmuson Foundation, which would become the state's greatest philanthropic foundation many years later.

When Davis and Renfrew took over NBA's legal business, some of the entanglements of small-town Anchorage became untangled. NBA, according to Fasnacht, had been relying upon lawyer and banker Warren Cuddy for legal services. This was somewhat unorthodox, since Cuddy was president of Anchorage's other large bank, First National Bank of Anchorage.

Fasnacht recalled the closeness of the two banks: "There was no competition between them. They agreed between them . . . who was going to loan the money to somebody and if the prices or the interest rate was exorbitant . . . there was no appeal because there was no other bank to go to."

Act of God?

Many lawyers who knew Bill Renfrew recall a person larger than life. In black-and-white photos from the 1940s he looks a bit like Errol Flynn with an impish smile and an expression just this side of a wink. It isn't surprising that those who shared his passions became his friends and brought him business. One of his greatest passions was flying.

People who got into airplane accidents, and their families, began to turn to Renfrew when their insurance companies refused to pay claims. Insurance companies often used the "act-of-God" defense which relieved them from paying the victim's family. As a pilot, Renfrew developed the ability to look at accident reports and determine whether God had really intervened, Fasnacht said. Eventually insurance companies decided they'd rather have Renfrew on their side than fight him in court and the firm added insurance defense to their line of work.

While Renfrew brought in the clients and, did much trial work, Davis did most of the office work and in the mid-1940s, so did John Hellenthal. But slogging through legal paperwork did not suit Hellenthal. Anchorage offered many more opportunities to a young man with ideas and energy. The thirty-year-old Hellenthal left Davis and Renfrew after only five months and stepped into territorial politics.

It wouldn't be until John Hughes joined Davis and Renfrew in the late 1940s that the firm found a man who enjoyed the office practice. Hughes eventually became the lead partner of Anchorage's biggest law firm of the latter part of the twentieth century. By then Ed Davis would be appointed to the Superior Court bench and Renfrew would be splitting his time between guiding, hunting, and practicing law.

Taking Up the Statehood Cause

Anchorage marched into the future with enthusiasm, listening to young people and urging the statehood movement forward. "They always elected young people to office," Hellenthal said, finding himself elected to the Constitutional Convention in 1955, the territorial legislature, and later the state legislature, all positions that helped him fashion the framework for the state of Alaska.

Again, Anchorage proved much different from Juneau where old-timers, according to Hellenthal, wouldn't listen to anyone, especially not to young people. "They did it all in secret and dropped little pearls of wisdom off on you," Hellenthal said. Not so in Anchorage, he added.

Here, young people made up the city council. The Junior Chamber of Commerce was very active and people listened to the members, Hellenthal said.

Although Hellenthal's choice to make Anchorage home proved provident, his view of Juneau is incomplete, especially when it comes to statehood.

Many strong proponents of statehood, including Mildred Hermann and Tom Stewart, both lawyers, made their home in Juneau. Both the Ketchikan and Juneau bar associations unanimously supported statehood proposals presented to Congress by Alaska delegate Anthony Dimond in the early 1940s.

Still, these voices are easily overshadowed in Hellenthal's mind by the most powerful lawyers he grew up among.

One of statehood's toughest opponents remained W. C. Arnold. Articulate and smart, Arnold—who at one time practiced law in Ketchikan—chaired the Alaska Salmon Industry, Inc., the trade association that opposed all efforts to tax the industry.

Hellenthal remembered that R. E. Robertson's opposition to statehood did not prevent him from being elected a delegate to the Constitutional Convention. Robertson actively worked on the judicial article—the article determining how judges would be appointed in the new state. However, when it came time to put his name to the document, Robertson refused. It was only later, when he was ill and near death, that Robertson was persuaded to sign the constitution, according to Hellenthal.

An even stronger opponent to statehood, according to Hellenthal, was H. L. Faulkner. "Faulkner, who probably made more money than any lawyer [in Juneau], fought statehood bitterly and sneakily, in a very underhanded fashion."

"Nobody likes taxes," Hellenthal said, acknowledging the perennial argument made against statehood. "But we wanted to show that we could take care of ourselves. That was a preliminary to statehood, and the anti-statehood people knew that. They didn't want us to ever become self-sufficient."

Hellenthal: Pugilistic and Old School Lawyer

Anchorage of the 1940s and 1950s provided Hellenthal what Juneau had given his father and uncle before him, a fresh start. The statehood movement provided a progressive agenda and forward-looking perspective. Hellenthal embraced the rhetoric of self-sufficiency that accompanied the statehood movement. It was a mantra he uttered easily. But as forward-looking and independent as Hellenthal considered himself politically, as a lawyer he put himself firmly in the less modern camp.

Hellenthal saved his charm for the public and election time. In the courtroom, his belligerent, obstreperous style earned him little respect. Although well educated, he chose to put on a show that was more blunderbuss than concrete law or facts.

Contemporaries of Hellenthal remember this dramatic style as common among old-time practitioners. "They think it's the way to win their cases," said John Dimond, the son of territorial judge Anthony Dimond. John Dimond, who later became an Alaska Supreme Court justice, remembered that Hellenthal could be "very biting" in court. He didn't care about anyone's feelings, said the mild-mannered Dimond.

Sarcastic comments flew between attorneys and quarrels erupted until the judge had to step in. Often the case got lost in accusations hurled back and forth among the attorneys.

Buell Nesbett, another lawyer who practiced in Anchorage in the 1940s and 1950s, and who at one time served as city magistrate, remembered hearing Hellenthal present a case in his court. Hellenthal was representing an owner of an Anchorage Fourth Avenue bar on some violation.

According to Nesbett, this was just one of many bars Hellenthal represented. On this occasion Hellenthal tried to rattle the judge by having what Nesbett called "all the village cowgirls" come to court. "It was supposed to get to me," Nesbett said. Nesbett, familiar with Hellenthal's tactics, remembered ruling against Hellenthal's client.

Hellenthal would not quarrel with these assessments of his legal style. He considered himself a liberal of the old school, offering his services equally—believing that any person who needs a lawyer deserves one. Hellenthal's clients included people whom he met while a carpenter on the base during World War II, along with those who owned the topless and bottomless bars situated only a few blocks east of his office and downtown.

As son of a territorial district judge and nephew to a well-respected Juneau mining attorney, Hellenthal held the pedigree of establishment in Juneau. On more than one occasion he had an opportunity to follow the more routine, steady practice of law—first in his uncle's office and later as an associate of Davis and Renfrew. He was drawn, instead, to a romantic notion of frontier Alaska, where individual style, rather than establishment pretensions and commercial ambitions, held sway.

Hellenthal's style would always be populist, his voice always raised for those with little power. Mavericks like Grigsby, Hellenthal, and later Wendell Kay, sustained an element of rebelliousness in a territorial bar. Their legal talents—especially in the case of Grigsby and Hellenthal—

were secondary to their persona. In the early years, they could get by on personality, on wits, but as the territory grew, so did expectations of what a lawyer should be.

Wendell Kay. Anchorage Bar Association, Oral History of Territorial Lawyers, Pamela Cravez. Joint archives of the Alaska Court System and the Alaska Bar Association.

8 ★
TALES
of the
SILVER
FOX

Wendell Kay, nearing age seventy when interviewed in 1982, sat in his thirteenth floor Anchorage law office overlooking the Chugach Mountains. Head of the firm Kay, Saville, Coffey, Hopwood & Schmid, and with a chair in his name at Arizona State University Law School, Kay had reached legendary status as Alaska's premier criminal trial lawyer.

He didn't sit still; he got up to walk around the room as he told stories. White haired, nearly six feet tall, lanky, with a loose-fitting suit, Kay appeared the quintessential country lawyer. Newspaper reporters had dubbed Kay the "Silver Fox," and he relished the characterization.

Kay didn't start out as a criminal trial lawyer. He pointed to a picture on the wall: it was this man, Kay said, who convinced him criminal trial work held the excitement he sought.

George Grigsby's twinkling eyes peered down from the keepsake photo bearing fifty-three signatures of past Anchorage bar members. "Grigsby received this commemorative picture on one of his birthdays," Kay recalled. The Anchorage bar routinely celebrated the event as a combination birthday and Christmas party.

"Have I told you the stories about Grigsby?" Kay asked.

George Grigsby. Framed photo signed by fifty-three members of the Anchorage bar. Presented to Grigsby on December 30, 1954, in honor of his eightieth birthday earlier that month, on December 2. Joint archives of the Alaska Court System and the Alaska Bar Association.

Eloquent, Sharp, Everything—A Star

In his rasping, softly persuasive voice, Kay described George Grigsby in his seventies, a giant among Anchorage trial lawyers. Six feet tall and 170 to 180 pounds at his normal fighting trim, the years had left him a little bent, Kay said. Still, Grigsby had a command and presence that made him the center of attention in court, and a wit that appealed to juror and judge. Grigsby was "totally well rounded," Kay said. "He knew the law, was eloquent, sharp, everything—a star."

Add a few pounds, not many, and Kay could have been describing himself. Kay, too, continued to enter the courtroom in the 1980s much as Grigsby had in the 1950s. Young trial lawyers vied to succeed Kay as the greatest criminal trial lawyer around. But he held them at bay with his bawdy, sharp wit and flamboyance, along with his familiarity to judge and jurors.

Kay began his first story about George Grigsby.

Marie Cox's Chili Parlor Story

George Grigsby was defending a man accused of stabbing another man in Marie Cox's Chili Parlor. The parlor, run by an outspoken Hispanic woman, was really a front for a house of prostitution, Kay said. While

Grigsby was cross-examining Marie Cox, "he got hooked up with the operation of the back door and he was asking Mrs. Cox if the back door opened into the house or out of the house."

"Well, in, Mr. Grigsby," she said.

He asked, "Is the doorknob on the right or the left," and so on.

"Finally, Mrs. Cox blew her stack and said, 'Mr. Grigsby, why are you asking me all these questions about the back door? You know that back door as well as I do, you're in and out of there every night.'"

"Grigsby just stood there looking at Mrs. Cox, smiling and nodding his head," Kay remembered. "I would have staggered over to the water pitcher and poured myself a glass and sat down.

"George just beamed at her and said, 'Why, of course, Mrs. Cox, you and I know all about that back door, but none of these fine gentlemen on the jury know anything about that back door.' And all of them were ducking and flinching, and everyone was laughing at them. . . . [Grigsby] never lost control, never lost his cool in the courtroom unless he wanted to."

Infectious Drama of Trials

From vastly different backgrounds, Grigsby and Kay met in Anchorage in the late 1940s. It was in Anchorage's courtrooms that each had his greatest success. Grigsby, having practiced in Alaska since the early 1900s, found the wartime boom and the economic opportunity elixirs for a fading career. When Kay, coming from a series of bureaucratic posts, saw Grigsby perform in court he awakened to the drama of criminal trial practice and soon flourished amid the "good ole boys" of an unregimented bar. As Grigsby's career waned Kay's waxed.

The criminal practice and carefree style of George Grigsby, the storytelling, the gambling, the lack of concern for other people's opinion, spurred Kay to abandon the more traditional law practice of his forebears in Watseka, Illinois.

Leaving "Arm's Length" Behind

Tall and slender, Kay had been very much unlike his athletic, barrel-chested father, who—according to Kay—always maintained a "teeny touch of arm's length" in the father-son relationship. The law firm of Kay and Kay, originating before the Civil War, had a respectable Midwestern image. Kay's father perpetuated the firm's reputation.

"He made money, made friends, was a man of substance," Kay said.

Respectability also meant avoiding criminal cases. The older Kay did handle one rape case, Kay remembered, and felt successful at keeping the sentence to ten years. Kay knew that he would follow his father into the family profession; however, he wasn't convinced his father's traditional business practice suited him.

After attending Northwestern University Law School and serving on its prestigious law review, Kay began a series of legal jobs—none of them having anything to do with criminal practice.

In 1938, straight out of law school, Kay went to Washington, DC, to work for the National Labor Relations Board. After a year he returned to Illinois and opened up an office with his brother in Centralia. Centralia had been a farming community, but when the two Kays opened their office it was enjoying an oil boom.

"Nobody knew one lawyer from another. We hung up a sign," said Kay. "As far as the average guy from Texas knew we were just as good lawyers as anybody else."

World War II interrupted the Kay brothers' partnership. And when the war was over, Wendell Kay had no desire to return to Illinois. He took a series of bureaucratic postings that finally led him to Alaska with the Alaska Housing Authority in 1946.

When he left the Housing Authority for private practice, Kay joined Paul Robison and Ralph Moody in one of Anchorage's first three-person partnerships. Robison handled real estate law, Moody contracted with the city of Anchorage to handle its affairs, and Kay represented Anchorage's utility districts, along with doing most of the firm's trial work.

There were only eighteen lawyers in Anchorage when Kay started making his civil appearances in court. He quickly gauged the competition and found the most able attorney on his feet was the old gold rush attorney, George Grigsby.

Kay vs. Grigsby

Kay remembered the first time he faced George Grigsby in court. Kay put his witness on the stand, examined him, and sat back for the cross-examination. Grigsby, with his pointed questioning, demolished the witness.

"I felt like crawling out of the courtroom," Kay said.

He received no consolation from Judge Folta, who presided over the case.

"I was in the library at recess, licking my wounds, and Judge Folta, who had tried many cases against George when they were in private practice in Juneau, said, 'Boy, George has certainly slipped, hasn't he?'

"I said, 'Slipped? Are you out of your mind? Why that old man is killing me.'

"He said, 'Well, you should have seen him 20 years ago.' I said, 'Thank God I wasn't practicing then.'"

Watching the finesse of Grigsby, Kay became enamored of the trial practice. Having both the education and the courtroom presence, he just needed experience. The freewheeling practice of the 1940s and 1950s gave it to him.

As Kay would later tell his trial advocacy students at Arizona State University, "Of the thousands of mistakes that a lawyer can make, I've made most of them, and therefore I can recognize them and try not to commit them again." But Kay had a kinder teacher than his mistakes. He had Grigsby.

Kay stayed in the background in the first case he and Grigsby handled together. Doing research and writing motions, handling a couple of witnesses, Kay watched Grigsby put together the presentation for the defendant, accused of first-degree murder.

Like a stage director, Grigsby subjected all the speaking parts to rigorous rehearsal. Kay marveled at Grigsby's meticulous preparation, remembering how Grigsby made sure the witnesses told their stories correctly and carefully, spending hours planning cross-examination. As a result, Grigsby's client got off with three years for homicide with the careless use of a firearm.

Gaining Trust and Prominence

Kay learned to appeal to the jurors' sensibilities. He gained their trust in the courtroom. In Anchorage of the 1940s and 1950s, the successful lawyer was a peer to his jurors. Kay's success in criminal trials rested on a heightened sense of what those in Anchorage were willing to tolerate or condone among their neighbors.

When people served on a jury, they either knew of Kay, or of his reputation. Kay derived great satisfaction from showing even his most loathsome client in a sympathetic light. Rather than presenting an obstacle, a particularly reprehensible client presented a challenge—to find just the right perspective that would gain a jury's sympathies.

Kay learned from Grigsby and other defense attorneys how to appeal to the chauvinist outlook in territorial Alaskans. The law that served Alaska, so their courtroom performances suggested, came from outside the community, and, when it came time to pass judgment, there was no better judge than a fellow Alaskan.

Politics and Criminal Law

Throughout the 1950s, Kay immersed himself in the affairs of Anchorage, the bar association, and Alaska. A vocal Democrat, he was elected to the territorial legislature, eventually serving as Speaker of the House; he became deeply involved in the statehood drive; and he was extremely active in the Anchorage and Alaska Bar Associations—helping with passage of the Integrated Bar Act in 1955.

Being a trial lawyer kept Kay sensitive to the pulse of his community, but it had its drawbacks. The public often associates trial lawyers with their clients. The greater Kay's reputation as a trial lawyer became, and the more heinous the crimes his clients were accused of committing, the more difficult it became for Kay to be elected to public office. Although he ran for office in the 1960s—at the height of his legal career—he could no longer win elections.

Entertainment and Notoriety

In the 1950s, Kay spent more and more of his time in the courtroom, his appetite for showmanship drawing him away from civil work and into the criminal trial arena.

Anchorage's courtroom in the 1940s and 1950s offered the excitement that people now find in movies or television. But not every case drew standing-room-only crowds. An enormous civil case might attract an audience of five while a criminal case would pack the courtroom.

"Criminal cases are where you get your notoriety," Kay observed in 1982. He remembered litigating one of the longest civil trials of the period, concerning a mining claim, and receiving the largest award up to that time, "and yet there weren't five people in the courtroom during the entire trial, and nothing in the newspapers."

But on a forgery case, known as the "Morrison-Knudsen check scandal," the courtroom was jammed every day of the trial, and big black headlines and photos made front-page news.

Check Scandal

Morrison-Knudsen Corporation, a construction firm that had built the Hoover (once known as Boulder) Dam in the 1930s and had become a prominent contractor with the US military during World War II, was a major construction employer in Alaska. In the 1950s, at the time of the check scandal, Morrison-Knudsen was involved in construction of the Distant Early Warning (DEW) Line of early radar stations in northern Canada and Alaska as well as White Alice Communications Systems in Alaska. Jimmy Ing, the prosecution claimed, forged two hundred Morrison-Knudsen checks and hired accomplices to pass the checks all over Alaska on a Labor Day weekend while the banks were closed.

The forged checks hurt Anchorage merchants, and the press covered the proceedings closely. The only evidence the state had against Ing was the accomplice's testimony. However, it is a basic legal doctrine that a person may not be convicted solely upon the uncorroborated testimony of an accomplice.

The enormous pressure from the public and the press, Kay said, made it impossible for Anchorage Federal District Court Judge J. L. McCarrey Jr. to dismiss the case.

The jury convicted Ing. Judge McCarrey gave him ten years on each of the twenty counts of forgery, the years to be served consecutively for two hundred years.

Kay remembered, "A little newspaper reporter said, 'Mr. Ing, 200 years, what in the world are you going to do?' Jimmy said, 'Well, it looks like I'll just have to do as much of it as I can.'"

As it turned out, Ing did not have to worry about completing the sentence. Kay wrote an appeal to the Ninth Circuit Court of Appeals in California, which reversed McCarrey's decision and dismissed the case.

Kay Battles Judge J. L. McCarrey Jr.

Kay, the master of nuance and courtroom sleight of hand, was a constant irritant to Third Judicial District Judge J. L. McCarrey Jr., who had come to Alaska first as a salesman for the Utah Woolen Mills, then went to law school in the 1940s and returned to practice. By many accounts, McCarrey's lack of flexibility and heightened sense of pomp and circumstance made him a difficult judge. Still, as one of the first Alaskan judges to wear a black robe in the courtroom, McCarrey looked like a judge and acquired some popularity with the public.

Although Kay could dance circles around McCarrey in terms of legal strategy and ability, Kay's steadily worsening drinking problem gave McCarrey, a strict Mormon, a wedge.

There were days when Kay would not make it into his office in time to make the scheduled early morning court appearance, and another lawyer would cover for him. Sometimes, though, that wasn't possible.

In one instance, remembered by then assistant US attorney James Fitzgerald, Kay had been out drinking the night before he was due in court and arrived the next morning with the lingering stale odor of tobacco and alcohol on him.

During the proceeding, Kay and opposing counsel George Boney were called to the bench for a conference with the judge. McCarrey, leaning over to talk to the two lawyers, smelled the stale odor of alcohol on Kay. Then US Attorney Fitzgerald reconstructed the exchange between attorneys.

"Mr. Kay have you been drinking? I think you've been drinking," McCarrey accused Kay.

"No, your honor," Kay replied.

Then McCarrey turned to Boney and asked him, "What do you think, Mr. Boney, has Mr. Kay been drinking, or hasn't he?"

"I don't think Mr. Kay is drunk, your honor," Boney said.

McCarrey, unsatisfied with either response, told Kay, "I'm going to send you down to Mr. Chenowith, report to Mr. Chenowith."

Chenowith, the territorial marshal, routinely gave sobriety tests to drivers. McCarrey instructed Chenoweth to report back to him on Kay's condition. Chenoweth, who some say saved "Kay's bacon," gave Kay a clean bill, which further frustrated McCarrey.

Discouraging and Expensive

Kay, fully aware of how his lifestyle alienated the judge, was equally irritated with the judge's unpredictable decisions and narrow interpretation of the law. Thirty years after appearing before the judge, Kay still simmers when retelling stories of his difficulties with McCarrey.

In the "Morrison-Knudsen check scandal" case, Kay said, Ing was charged with a crime for which there was no adequate evidence. The lawyers argued that the territory prohibited trying a man only on the uncorroborated testimony of an accomplice. But McCarrey refused to listen, Kay said.

"That's discouraging and it's expensive," Kay continued. Similar things happened in "case after case, both civil and criminal, just bad law. When you're up against a situation like that, it's hard to predict what's going to happen. You tell your client he has a good case, but don't know what Judge McCarrey might do to it."

Sporting Theory of Justice

More than personality separated Kay from Judge McCarrey. Their confrontations came from the character of Alaska law.

A number of Anchorage lawyers at the time didn't impose very heavy restrictions on themselves. They went as far as they could, often crossing into territory that today would be cause for disciplinary action. But in the 1950s, it became a demonstration of cleverness. Tricks lawyers played on one another turned into something to laugh about. But not every lawyer in the 1950s found the situation humorous.

"That older group manipulated the courts in scheduling, witnesses, evidence, just about anything they could get away with. . . . There was more of a sporting contest, a sporting theory of justice. Lawyers were considered to be even more free to be total, unabashed advocates then than they are today. Then, they didn't have nearly the professional conduct obligation that the court now expects," observed John Rader, who started practicing in Alaska in the early 1950s and became Alaska's first attorney general.

As the lawyers were free to be unabashed advocates, the power of federal district judges to decide in any manner they thought appropriate was equally unrestrained, except in very rare cases. Only the Ninth Circuit Court of Appeals in San Francisco could overrule the Alaska District Court, and that involved an expensive appeal and a trip to San Francisco. Even then, the appeals court judges viewed Alaskan lawyers with skepticism and tended to side with the Alaskan judge.

In the 1950s, as Alaska headed toward statehood, McCarrey's and Kay's struggles highlighted the problems of relying upon the territorial courts to settle legal conflicts.

Kay, an expert in trial practice, faced a judge from an office practice with little litigation experience. Responsive to the public's demand for an effective court system that would prepare the territory for statehood, McCarrey sought to hold the court and the lawyers who practiced before it to a higher standard. But McCarrey's lack of litigation experience and inflexibility had the opposite effect, diminishing his ability to make any changes. Kay, at ease both with the character of trial practice and with the character of the territory, took advantage of a less rigorous justice system to further his clients' causes.

You Are What People Think You Are, Whether You Want to Be or Not

Kay's flamboyance made for good press and, time after time, his success before juries, particularly in criminal cases, became legendary. As one territorial lawyer put it, Kay "was a good trial lawyer. He would take almost any kind of case. He really wasn't very selective in his cases. The press picked this up. They would abuse him at times about it."

But it built Kay's reputation, and it built Kay's perception of himself as a criminal trial attorney. "If the press, who develops favorites, creates legends and augments them, points to you, then the next thing you know, *you* are what people think you are, whether you want to be or not," Rader said. Although Kay was an astute civil as well as criminal litigator, by the end of the 1950s, his reputation was that of a criminal attorney.

Kay observed the trappings of being known as a criminal trial lawyer. First, criminal trial lawyers are known by their first name, and he was known to all as "Wendell." Second, it made little difference who a criminal trial lawyer represented.

"He could represent Adolph Hitler, Genghis Khan, the Boston Axe Murderer, and it wouldn't hurt his practice," remarked Kay. "There might be a few people who say, 'I don't want to go to him, he represents those awful people,' but there would be other people who'd say, 'Gee, we'd better get him, he must be good, look what he did for that axe murderer.'"

Fearful Father

Kay was most renowned for his handling of murder cases—getting people off in a pinch. The death penalty was in effect in Alaska for murder until 1957, and it used to be claimed "that nobody could consider themselves a trial lawyer unless they had defended someone accused of murder," Kay said. Kay handled between fifty and a hundred murder cases throughout his career. Only one of his clients was ever convicted of first-degree murder, and there the death penalty was not imposed. These tough cases had an allure for Kay.

"I believe I'm required to defend people who ask me to represent them. I've always made it a habit of taking whatever cases came to me, if they were able to pay a reasonable fee and if they wanted me to represent them, regardless of what they did or regardless of how heinous the situation might be, and how unforgivable the conduct might be." Kay took delight in winning the jury over to his side, seducing it on his client's behalf.

Kay managed to sway a jury in one case in which even the client's father, who was paying Kay's fee, was so afraid of his son that he testified against him in court. The young man had been accused of stabbing a woman to death. He stabbed her thirty-seven times while her eight-year-old daughter huddled under the bedcovers in the next room.

"Horrible," Kay observed, then added, "The question, of course, was whether or not [the client] was the right man." Was it the client's buddy or the client who actually committed the murder? Even in the face of testimony from the boy's father, Kay managed to put enough doubt in the jurors' minds to get the boy off the first degree murder charge.

Wife Kills Husband in His Sleep

Well before the "battered wife syndrome" was even coined in court, Wendell Kay pitched the defense for Mary Lee Allison. Allison was accused of murdering her husband, Bill, in his sleep.

Bill had repeatedly beaten Mary Lee and threatened their infant daughter. He was also addicted to a popular nonprescription cough medicine that contained codeine.

One night, Bill arrived home in a rage, beat Mary Lee, threatened to kill her in the morning, and fell asleep under the influence of the codeine cough medicine.

Covered with bruises, Mary Lee took a gun and shot out the back of Bill's head.

Kay admitted that "there was really no defense. . . . She had intentionally and willfully and deliberately shot her husband and killed him while he lay in bed sound asleep."

Still, Kay, looking beyond the legal technicalities, concluded that Mary Lee did a "very fine thing." She saved her life and the life of her child, and "removed a vicious, worthless character from the face of the earth. Instead of being punished, she should have been rewarded."

Kay impressed upon the district attorney the likelihood that no jury would ever convict a woman for doing what Allison had done to her husband under the circumstances. The district attorney, finally won over, asked the grand jury to come back with the reduced charge of manslaughter.

Kay pled his client guilty to the manslaughter charge, knowing that Judge Ralph Moody, who had been partners with Kay in the 1950s, had a "distinct admiration for beautiful women."

Allison, a striking redhead, was sentenced to three years on probation, which was later reduced to one year. She served a one-year probation for what had originally been a first degree murder charge.

"Didn't Used to Be Quite This Peaceful"

"Defending somebody and approving of their conduct are two different things," Kay said. "I don't like the idea of people shooting or hurting each other in any way. I am a very calm peaceful man. At least now. I didn't used to be quite this peaceful."

By the mid-1950s, Kay had mastered the "beautiful final arguments" and "devastating cross-examination" for which he'd admired Grigsby; he also had acquired the entire style—the hard drinking, hard living, convivial excitement—of the territorial litigator. The pace of the 1950s and the demands of his trial practice punished him.

"Trial practice is a strenuous occupation. Many people don't appreciate how intense the labor of a trial lawyer is," Kay said, as looked back on his career. "You tend to exclude everything else from your life while you're trying a case, except the case. Your family, kids, other work at the office, you don't answer the telephone, you don't look at anything. You quit reading the newspaper. So, when the thing is over, there's a tremendous letdown, and, besides that, Alaska is a great drinking country. So, there's a tremendous inclination to get drunk because you won. Or because you lost. Or just get drunk because it's 'St. Swithen's Day,' or for any reason. Unless you watch it, the next thing you know is you're having a battle with the bottle."

And Kay did battle. Although Kay made much money, he also spent great sums. And the collapse of his home life culminated in a divorce from his wife, the mother of his five children.

Silver Fox

As Grigsby had become the old-time crafty trial attorney from gold rush days for the Anchorage bar of the 1940s, Kay became the wily "Silver Fox" of the 1960s and 1970s. Whether beguiling judge and juror well aware of his reputation, or telling his stories of an earlier Alaska law practice, Kay evoked the nostalgia and continuity so important to Alaskans who love the legend and fear the fading of their frontier.

It was not difficult to ascertain in the late 1940s that Alaska was prime territory for the legend of the trial lawyer. After Grigsby, there were none better qualified than Wendell Kay to fill that role. Well educated and willing to learn the game of territorial practice, he crossed the generational line among Alaska lawyers. His manner and method joined him to that old group of attorneys who slowly faded after statehood, but, unlike them, he survived the transition to the modern practice of the 1960s and 1970s.

In the late 1950s, Roger Cremo, secretary of the Anchorage Bar Association, wrote the eightyish Grigsby, then president of the Anchorage bar, that the president would no longer receive a salary. No more money would be forthcoming from that association to aid the financially unstable Grigsby.

As Kay entered his seventh decade, he had partners and a firm that provided steady income, taught during the Alaska winter at the University of Arizona Law School where a "chair" had been established in his name, and still counted himself the retired, undefeated heavyweight drinking champion of the bar.

Kay also recognized, just as Grigsby before him, that up-and-coming contenders would always be vying for the title.

George Folta with slain wolf. Richard C. Folta, "Of Bench and Bears: Alaska's Bear Hunting Judge," Great Northwest Publishing and Distributing, 1986.

9 ★

Judge George FOLTA: License TO HUNT

While many lawyers enjoyed Alaska's less structured professional environment, one that allowed for short work days, novel court arguments, and an informal manner, other lawyers regarded the laid-back frontier practice with suspicion. These attorneys considered Alaska's legal climate in great need of order, rules, and structure. This attitude was particularly prevalent among lawyers working in government positions, such as in the US attorney's office, the Department of Interior solicitor's office, and among some judges.

Many young lawyers who began their careers as avid prosecutors, eager to prove their worth in court and add convictions to their record, mellowed over the years and later blended into the easy camaraderie of territorial attorneys. Others, like George Folta, became hardened in their conviction that the frontier demanded vigilance and strong-armed justice.

George Folta: Bear-Hunting Judge

George Folta's passion for bear hunting is remembered by nearly all those who tell stories about the man appointed district judge for the Second Division in southeast Alaska in 1947.

Reputed to have killed around two hundred bears, more than any other Alaskan, Folta would stalk his prey through the woods, waiting until the very last moment, when the animal was in full charge, and then shoot. Judge Folta's presence in the courtroom during criminal trials was very similar to his comportment on bear hunts. Sitting in judgment, he'd wait for the prosecutor to flush out the defendant. If the prosecutor didn't do his job well enough, Folta would join in the hunt, framing questions for the prosecutor, completing the case, and finally, staging the kill with a damning look.

A skillful courtroom manipulator, Folta maddened defense attorneys in the 1940s and 1950s with his facial expressions, suggesting sympathy with the prosecution. That such indications never appeared on the trial record made appeals especially tricky. After a particularly egregious instance, Bailey Bell, a perennial plaintiff's personal injury attorney, appealed down to the Ninth Circuit.

"I love Judge Folta as much as one man can honorably love another," the effusive ex-Oklahoman reputedly declared to the circuit court, "but he was prejudiced."

The Ninth Circuit rarely reversed Folta.

Born in 1893, the son of an immigrant coal miner from Eastern Europe, Folta attended school in Washington State where he developed a lifelong love of the wilderness. He went to Beutel Business College in Tacoma and learned shorthand at the urging of his mother, who wanted her son to have a vocation before he left home. Folta's passion for the outdoors and hunting led him to Ketchikan in 1912, arriving when he was nineteen years old. The shorthand skill helped him get his first job in the US Steamship Inspection Service. He also began to hunt bears, taking his first trip to Kodiak.

In 1915, Folta moved to Juneau to work for Governor John F. A. Strong and then as secretary to Strong's successor, Governor Thomas Riggs. In the Juneau court clerk's office, he worked his way up to reporter, read legal cases, and eventually entered the practice of law without ever attending a day of law school. This journeyman approach to the law gave him something in common with his closest friend and mentor in the Juneau bar, H. L. Faulkner.

A strict sense of personal discipline attended Folta's demeanor, and that sense served him through more than forty years of government work.

Folta served in the US attorney's office for a number of years and became known as an aggressive prosecutor. In 1939, he sought and received a death verdict in a case from Ketchikan against Nelson Charles, a Native American. Charles was the first man hanged by the

Seaborn Buckalew in uniform in the 1960s. Joint archives of the Alaska Court System and the Alaska Bar Association.

district court in Juneau in the twentieth century. Between 1900 and 1957, when the death penalty was abolished in Alaska, eight men were executed. Folta served as either prosecutor or judge in the cases involving the last three men to be executed, beginning with Nelson Charles in 1939.

In addition to being a prosecutor, Folta served as solicitor for the Department of the Interior. In 1947, he was appointed judge for the First Division. His reputation as a prosecutor on the bench preceded him wherever he traveled.

The Anchorage jails emptied out at the suggestion that Judge Folta would be coming up from Juneau to help Third Division District Judge Anthony Dimond with his caseload. Defense lawyers urged clients to change their pleas rather than face Folta's construction of the law. Prosecutors, though, rallied around this nemesis to errant defendants.

Sheep Hunting with the Prosecutor

Seaborn Buckalew, an assistant US attorney in Anchorage during Folta's term, would request Judge Folta come up from his Juneau post to preside over Anchorage matters. Buckalew, who would later be appointed to the Superior Court in Anchorage and retire as a colonel in the National Guard, found that Folta reminded him of a marine sergeant. Perhaps recognizing a kindred spirit, Folta invited Buckalew and another attorney on a sheep-hunting trip on one of his visits to Anchorage.

Buckalew remembered the trip with some chagrin, comparing it to a forced march through miles of wilderness.

In an effort to find better hunting grounds, the judge directed his companions to ford the rough, unpredictable, and glacier-fed Matanuska River. Hours later, with still no sheep in sight, the trio returned to the river. Warm weather had made the water rise to a dangerous level. The other lawyer and Buckalew tried to dissuade Folta from crossing at their original point, but the judge, in his fifties and more than a couple of decades older than his companions, plunged into the murky waters. He collapsed fighting the fierce current and the two others had to dive into the freezing water after him. Packs and guns weighed them down, but the three somehow managed to make it to the other side.

Although US attorneys usually preferred Folta as trial judge, astute criminal defense attorneys also knew how to appeal to this transparent jurist.

Folta's Blind Spots

Buckalew remembered one sentencing hearing for a man convicted of assault with a dangerous weapon where a clever Anchorage defense attorney—Stanley McCutcheon—countered the prosecutor's demand for a stiff sentence by recounting the client's wartime service.

Mr. Randall, pointed out McCutcheon, had been a sergeant in the infantry during World War II and had received the Silver Star for his part in the seizing of the strategic Ludendorff Bridge during the battle of Remagen. Everyone had depended upon Sergeant Randall: the French general who had 450 tanks that needed to get over the bridge, Randall's own infantry division, and General Eisenhower sitting back at the big headquarters. When Randall finally secured the Remagen bridge, tanks rolled into Germany, soldiers rolled into Germany, and Sergeant Randall was the one who made all that possible.

Judge Folta paid close attention "to this nonsense," remembered Buckalew. By the time attorney McCutcheon got around to telling the judge how President Eisenhower had pinned the Silver Star and

General De Gaulle, the Croix de Guerre, on Randall, Buckalew knew that the sentence would be lenient. And it was.

Folta's blind spots—an admiration for government service, loyalty, and duty—could influence his judgment. During his lengthy government career, Folta's philosophical nature changed little: he remained dedicated to bringing order to the frontier and using the bench as a prosecutorial tool. Discipline and steely attention to detail served him throughout his life, from daily walks on the streets of Juneau to his frequent bear hunts.

In 1955, after spending a week in Anchorage handling cases, Folta returned home to Juneau and then flew with friends to Yakutat for a bear hunt. On a cold spring morning, Folta sat in the front of the sixteen-foot dory, bent over to bail water that had splashed in, and suffered a fatal heart attack.

US District Court for the District of Alaska Judge James Fitzgerald. Anchorage Bar Association, Oral History of Territorial Lawyers, Pamela Cravez. Joint archives of the Alaska Court System and the Alaska Bar Association.

10 ★
Remembering Judge FOLTA AND Ketchikan's Red Light DISTRICT

James Fitzgerald arrived in Ketchikan as an assistant US attorney in 1952. In 1982, he remembered Ketchikan's gun-toting police chief who had plans to go into business with a local prostitute, the city magistrate with a habit of passing bad checks, and Judge George Folta's determination to clean up Ketchikan's "tolerated" red light district.

Balding, with the stocky build of an ex-football player, Fitzgerald sat in his federal district court office, Alaska history books filled the bookcases and photos of Alaska jurists from statehood lined the walls, reminders of his long and distinguished career. Appointed to the Superior Court after statehood, then to the Alaska Supreme Court in 1972, and finally, the Federal District Court bench in 1974, Fitzgerald had a keen appreciation for how much the practice of law had evolved since he began practicing law in Alaska.

Fitzgerald came to Alaska in the early 1950s expecting to find the excitement and color described by his father, who had followed the gold rush trail in the early 1900s from Skagway all the way to St. Michael near Nome. James Fitzgerald found little of that excitement on his first job with a logging company in Ketchikan. Just out of law school and awaiting the results of the Oregon bar exam, Fitzgerald was not charmed by rainy, wet Ketchikan and was not much looking forward to the practice of law.

He left for a year to go to graduate law school, then grudgingly decided to try the town again when he got a job as assistant US attorney. This time Fitzgerald would find the "wild west" he'd been looking for.

Creek Street Bawdy Houses and One-Armed Bandits

Sitting in his government office in 1952, Assistant US Attorney Fitzgerald had a clear view of Creek Street. The wooden walkway ran upstream from the boat harbor and was lined with nearly every brothel in Ketchikan. Deputy marshals, who were in charge of investigating crimes and making arrests both outside town boundaries and within them, when necessary, informed Fitzgerald that prostitution had been allowed for a long time in Ketchikan.

The town of 5,000 had its own police chief and officers who operated a business-like approach to prostitution. Prostitutes were allowed uptown on Thursday afternoons and had to work for madams in one of the houses on Creek Street.

Gambling also flourished in Ketchikan. "If you paid for a drink in a bar with a five-dollar bill, the bartender returned all your change in silver coins. Slot machines were everywhere . . . in bars, in fraternal clubs, in downtown stores, and in bawdy houses. The Elks Club, carrying a large mortgage, featured several one-armed bandits on its premises," Fitzgerald recalled. And to make things easier for gamblers, Ketchikan restaurants and bars accepted silver dollars as the preferred legal tender.

Fitzgerald, completely responsible for the US attorney's office since his boss, Patrick Gilmore, spent the bulk of his time in Juneau, worried about the lax enforcement of what normally would have been illegal offenses. Fitzgerald called Gilmore and asked for instructions.

Gilmore, born in Ketchikan in 1911, was accustomed to the city's idiosyncrasies. His father and uncle had arrived in Ketchikan at the turn of the century from Ireland and had flourished. Patrick's father built the Gilmore Hotel in the 1920s and served as mayor in the 1930s. Gilmore was also well educated in the law, receiving his law degree from Georgetown University in 1938. His familiarity with Ketchikan and his legal background made him a great favorite among jurors.

Gilmore reassured Fitzgerald that the Department of Justice did not dictate local policy on gambling and prostitution, but cooperated with town officials in the enforcement of whatever policy they chose.

Fitzgerald observed later that while Alaska was a territory, federal agencies within it functioned pretty much as they pleased. Although technically US attorneys were responsible for enforcing all laws on the books—federal, territorial, and city ordinances—in practice, Fitzgerald would, per US Attorney Gilmore, defer to local policy.

Ketchikan Legal System

Despite its tolerance of prostitution and gambling and other quirks, Ketchikan's local legal system seemed to hum along just fine. Ketchikan's commissioner, Katherine Davenport, handled misdemeanors and minor offenses with much common sense and no legal training. The city magistrate had legal training, a drinking habit, and a propensity for passing bad checks. It was considered a good joke on the magistrate to assign one of his bad checks to pay any fine he imposed in court, Fitzgerald remembered.

District Court Judge Folta traveled to Ketchikan twice a year, coinciding with the ebb and flow of commerce and activity. A bustling summer fishing and logging season was followed by Judge Folta coming down in the fall to handle criminal cases. He'd convene a grand jury during which the US attorney would present cases. Indictments coming out of the grand jury set the pace for the fall's criminal calendar.

In the spring, Judge Folta traveled to Ketchikan to handle civil matters.

This all went along smoothly until Ketchikan got a new police chief who decided to clean up the red light district.

Police Chief and the "Prairie Chicken"

In 1953, Del Freimuth took over as police chief. Fitzgerald remembered Freimuth as one of the strangest men he'd ever met. Fascinated by guns, Freimuth loved to wear them and talk about them. When Fitzgerald and Freimuth sat through a western movie together, Freimuth constantly interrupted the action to analyze the gunmen's quick draws.

Fitzgerald wasn't alone in his concern. Police officers under his command found Freimuth's handling of guns to be homicidal. He'd carry four or five guns at a time, even going so far as to threaten citizens and fellow officers with them.

Although his only background in law enforcement was in providing piloting services for the Fish and Wildlife Enforcement Agency, Freimuth enjoyed strong local support.

Freimuth told Fitzgerald he was going to put the prostitution line out of business and placed an officer at the entrance to the boardwalk to Creek Street. This dissuaded more well-known townspeople from frequenting the brothels.

Eager to advertise his progress, Freimuth brought the city manager down to Creek Street to show him that it was out of business. The "Prairie Chicken," an elderly madam on the line, hearing the footsteps on the boardwalk and hopeful of business, opened her door. Failing to recognize the police chief and city manager, she offered them the services of her house.

"The city manager was so outraged he turned on his heels and stalked off. He wouldn't even get in the police vehicle with Freimuth," recalled Fitzgerald.

Although Freimuth professed to be "cleaning up" the prostitution business, it began to look like he was taking over the business. Fitzgerald learned that Freimuth was arranging for new girls coming to town to check first with the police, take a physical, and give a personal history before being directed to Creek Street. Not only was he attempting to go into business with a prostitute, the married Freimuth was also having an affair with one. When Fitzgerald confronted Freimuth, he was told it was none of the assistant US attorney's concern. The police chief's affairs were private.

Freimuth's indiscretions disturbed Fitzgerald, but even more disturbing was the police chief's inability to train his officers.

Fitzgerald remembered going to court on prostitution cases and learning midtrial that undercover vice officers had never been instructed that it was just as unlawful for them to engage in acts of prostitution with the women as it was for the women. Between illegal police actions and mishandled evidence, Fitzgerald found it nearly impossible to enforce federal law.

Ketchikan's Reformers Bend Judge Folta's Ear

It wasn't long before the police chief's actions became fodder for Ketchikan's growing group of civic reformers. The reformers, led by Emery Tobin, publisher of the *Alaska Sportsman*, complained to the

Judge Folta. Richard C. Folta, "Of Bench and Bears: Alaska's Bear Hunting Judge," Great Northwest Publishing and Distributing, 1986.

Department of Justice about the lack of prosecution for gambling and prostitution offenses and gained Judge Folta's ear.

In the meantime, Freimuth left and Ketchikan got a new police chief. But this did not stop Tobin from continuing to complain to the judge. This time, according to Fitzgerald, Tobin told Judge Folta that the new police chief's wife had been a prostitute, inferring that once again the police would be ignoring Ketchikan's prostitution business.

Fitzgerald believed Tobin's accusations unjust, still, the publisher's influence was enough to make Judge Folta travel to Ketchikan and take the matter into his own hands.

Folta: This Is a Showdown

When Judge Folta convened the grand jury in Ketchikan in 1953, it was with the purpose of cleaning up Ketchikan's illegal prostitution business. Not only would it validate Folta's power as judge and his strong sense of order, but it would also prove to the Department of Justice that no other judge could be quite as effective as he at reining in the frontier. With

President Eisenhower's election that year, all territorial officials, from district judge and US attorney to commissioner, would be subject to dismissal to allow the new Republican administration their appointments.

Fitzgerald, who had gone through the formalities of getting Democratic Party approval for his post a year earlier, expected to be replaced, as did his boss, US Attorney Gilmore. Judge Folta had no intention of being replaced, according to Fitzgerald.

Folta began, according to Fitzgerald, by instructing the Ketchikan grand jury that it was to investigate fearlessly and independently, implying that it was not to be influenced by prosecutors or law enforcement officials. The judge then left for Juneau, leaving the grand jury to its work.

Normally, prosecutors assist the grand jury, presenting cases and directing their inquiries so that the resulting indictments are substantiated with adequate facts and cases may go smoothly on to trial. Folta, by his instructions, signaled that this grand jury should not trust those presenting cases.

Fitzgerald's boss, US Attorney Patrick Gilmore, had come down to Ketchikan with Folta to present cases to the grand jury with Fitzgerald's assistance. The grand jury began to call Creek Street madams to testify, exposing all of Freimuth's inept dealings, including encouraging girls to work for only certain madams. The grand jury also learned of Freimuth's affair with a prostitute.

US Attorney Gilmore, remembered Fitzgerald, was very unsympathetic to the questioning of the women. He spent little time with their testimony and seemed impatient with what was becoming a fishing expedition into the personal morals of the ex-police chief, rather than a clearly focused inquiry into criminal activity.

Fitzgerald sensed the grand jury's growing hostility toward Gilmore's slack presentation, but before Gilmore had a chance to act on Fitzgerald's hunch, the jury foreman asked both Gilmore and Fitzgerald to stay out of the courtroom.

For two weeks the grand jury operated independently, and rumors flew about town. Finally, the foreman called Judge Folta, who arrived on the afternoon flight. At seven that evening, the foreman delivered the grand jury's unanimous recommendation that the new "acting" police chief be charged with obstructing justice, and US Attorney Gilmore be removed from the proceedings.

Gilmore sprang to his feet and asked for an opportunity to respond, but Folta cut him off.

"This is a showdown," Folta said, according to Fitzgerald.

Ketchikan's "local policy" no longer applied. Under Folta's direction the Ketchikan grand jury struck out on its own, endorsing a new intolerance for prostitution, gambling, and bootlegging.

Folta directed Fitzgerald to take over and prepare a complaint against the new police chief for obstructing justice. When Fitzgerald asked how he should go about filling in the information, Folta became very short and just said to prepare the charge.

A complaint must normally allege that a person obstructed justice in some specific way, but Folta directed Fitzgerald to ignore this requirement and just write a general complaint charging the new police chief with obstructing justice. And there was to be no bond.

Whenever the grand jurors thought Fitzgerald was not being helpful enough, they called Judge Folta to intervene.

In one instance the grand jury requested that Fitzgerald file an information—a charge against a person—but they did not tell him what statute they thought had been violated. When he asked the jurors to be more specific, they told him to wait, so they could call Judge Folta.

Folta, on the telephone, intimated that the Department of Justice had been checking up on Fitzgerald. The veiled threat was not lost on the young assistant US attorney.

"Right then I felt like saying to hell with it," Fitzgerald remembered. But he stuck it out.

When the grand jury finished, it found corruption within the Ketchikan Police Department, including Police Chief Del Freimuth's complicity with the Creek Street prostitution business, gambling businesses, and bootlegging. The grand jury found that the police not only tolerated the outlawed businesses, but also frequented them, and in some cases protected them from planned raids.

The grand jury also found that city officials were derelict in their duty to suppress vice and corruption. Regarding US Attorney Gilmore, the grand jury alleged Gilmore obstructed justice and recommended his removal. Although the allegations referred to Gilmore's failure to prosecute cases, it did not specify which cases. The report did find that prostitutes got too light a fine in commissioner's court, or weren't prosecuted vigorously, and that Gilmore's presentation to the grand jury was inadequate.

As soon as the grand jury finished its term, Fitzgerald left Ketchikan for the Juneau office of the US attorney. Another assistant US attorney was sent down to try the cases presented by the grand jury.

Both Fitzgerald and Folta retained their positions through the change in presidential administrations. No charges were brought against Gilmore. He returned to private practice, though the grand jury report left a lasting sting.

Lasting Consequences

Judge Folta's tendency to overlook the law in order to pursue ends he desired was not confined to cases involving prostitution and gambling. Nor was Judge Folta the only territorial Alaska judge bending the law to serve his own ends. Territorial attorneys became accustomed to appearing before judges who had their own agendas. Attorneys adapted their arguments depending upon the jurist. But they had little recourse when that failed.

In the 1950s more well-educated lawyers like Buckalew and Fitzgerald began practicing in Alaska. These lawyers, who often began as prosecutors, understood the government point of view and also the need for more predictability in the law. Tolerance for the one-sided power of judges diminished. Judge Folta's strong-arm tactics of manipulating jury trials and grand juries would have lasting consequences. Especially as he was joined on the bench by J. L. McCarrey Jr., appointed by President Eisenhower in 1955 to be district court judge for the Third Division.

Tensions were growing between the bench and bar and would soon boil over.

11 ★

Influence and Discipline: POLICING Territorial Lawyers

A lawyer is an officer of the court—a minister in the temple . . . of justice. His high calling demands of him fidelity to his clients with an eye single to their best interests, as well as good faith and honorable dealings with the courts and the public in general.

—Judge J. L. McCarrey Jr.

In retrospect, Arthur David "Dave" Talbot would have handled things differently. When interviewed thirty years after the *Stringer* case went to court in 1953, he admitted he made a mistake. He should never have taken charges against Anchorage attorney Herald Stringer to the grand jury. Talbot confessed that he always seemed to take the wrong side, or too serious a view of conduct among attorneys when he was an assistant US attorney in Anchorage. Looking back, he observed that those territorial lawyers might have appeared informal, but "when you get underneath that, these were tremendous people."

Talbot, the son of an Episcopal pastor, grew up on a Ute Indian reservation in Utah, where his father ran a mission. He served in the US Navy and worked in a Wall Street law firm before taking a position in the US attorney's office in Anchorage in 1952.

Talbot, recalled defense attorney Edgar Paul Boyko, had a gung-ho attitude, running around with a six-shooter strapped to his side, staking out the Last Chance Bar for morals violations with the assistant deputy marshal.

Dave Talbot with Buell Nesbett's son, Walt, in the 1950s. Courtesy Walt Nesbett.

Dave Talbot when interviewed in August 1982. Anchorage Bar Association Oral History of Territorial Lawyers, Pamela Cravez. Joint archives of the Alaska Court System and the Alaska Bar Association.

Prosecutors had the "juice"—the power to decide who would be prosecuted for a crime and who would not. Each prosecutor had a card that allowed him to enter any bar or house in town, on a raid or otherwise, and they often accompanied marshals on raids.

Given all this power, it wasn't unusual for defense attorneys to scope out new arrivals in the prosecutor's office. Young prosecutors were invited to bar lunches, where they were wined and dined and regaled with frontier stories. On the pretext of being helpful, defense attorneys often offered to chauffeur new assistant US attorneys around town. The highlight of the tour was always Eastchester Flats, a hotbed of gambling and prostitution.

As the young prosecutor got a look at Anchorage's rougher neighborhood, the chauffeuring attorney made much of his acquaintance with the new "juice" among the steady clientele from the area.

Until he'd seen Eastchester Flats for himself, Talbot had the impression that Anchorage's rougher element all lived in one tremendous skyscraper in the middle of the Flats at Eighteenth and Karluk, since nearly every criminal defendant gave this intersection as their place of residence.

In fact, Eastchester Flats was a mirror neighborhood of Westchester, both of which bordered Chester Creek, which flowed from the mountains to Cook Inlet. Westchester, on the Cook Inlet side of the Creek, housed Anchorage's affluent, while Eastchester, tucked under the Chugach Mountain side of the Creek, was home to Anchorage's red light district, nightclubs, restaurants, after-hours bars, and gambling dens.

Eastchester Flats attracted the city's lawyers, politicians, and council members, as well as soldiers from the nearby bases, to its rib joints and entertainment establishments. The area, which is now home to the Anchorage Senior Center and intersected by the Seward Highway, was called the "Valley of Ten Thousand Smokes," due to the many marijuana dealers. Some police officers derogatorily referred to the mostly black neighborhood as "Cadillac Row," for the big cars driven by local pimps.

In the 1950s, Eastchester Flats was merely a dirt road lined with wooden shacks and trees and places with names like the Lark, the Harlem Club, the Mermaid, the Chicken Shack, Red Hut, and North Starlight Lounge.

Of course, crime in Anchorage was not confined to Eastchester Flats. And the prosecutors' power to enforce laws extended beyond criminal complaints. One additional area where prosecutors had discretionary power was in their response to complaints against lawyers.

Many places outside of Alaska had integrated bar associations, where a state gives the authority to regulate the legal profession to a state bar association. This authority includes developing the rules and requirements for membership, ethical standards, and general responsibility for maintaining professional standards among practicing attorneys. This includes handling complaints against attorneys.

In 1953, Alaska did not have an integrated bar association. Instead, the territory had bar examiners who administered the bar exam and graded it, although territorial lawyers remember there being some inconsistencies in the results. Complaints against attorneys were often handled by the US attorney's office. The office would investigate, and if it found an offense, it would take the matter to the grand jury for indictment. Once a grand jury indicted, the matter would go to the territorial court for adjudication.

When former taxi driver Robert Kemp walked into Assistant US Attorney Dave Talbot's office to complain about the exorbitant fee he'd been charged by his attorney, Herald Stringer, Talbot listened carefully and then made his first mistake.

The Cost of a White Slavery Defense

In the early morning hours of May 6, 1952, Robert Kemp was dispatched by the Radio Cab Company to pick up a woman who needed a ride. When she got into his cab, the woman told Kemp to go to the Alley Cat Bar, on C Street between Fourth and Fifth Avenues downtown. There she told him to stop and pick up three soldiers, who then got into the cab with her. As Kemp began to drive toward Mountain View and the east side of town, the woman slumped out of sight. Just as he asked her to sit up an Anchorage police officer pulled the cab over.

Kemp was jailed and arrested for "white slavery," the term for transporting a woman for the purpose of prostitution.

While he was in jail, the owner of the cab company who had dispatched Kemp visited him in jail and brought a lawyer, Herald Stringer, who offered to defend Kemp.

It is here where questions begin to arise over how much Stringer charged to represent Kemp and whether his fee included paying for Stringer's political "influence" with the judge and justice system.

Kemp says that while he was still in jail he agreed to pay Stringer $500 for the entire case.

Stringer testified that it was only when Kemp came to his office later with the owner of the cab company that they agreed to his fee for the case: $2,500.

Whether the fee was $500 or $2,500, Kemp didn't have the money. He began to look around for another lawyer who would charge less. He found one who would charge just $250.

As he was getting ready to tell Stringer he no longer needed his services, the owner of the cab company convinced Kemp to reconsider, "since Mr. Stringer was politically powerful and could best handle the case."

Kemp, who had never been involved in a criminal action before, continued to see Stringer on the advice of the cab company owner. Kemp testified that he believed the $2,500 fee would only be charged if the case were dismissed, but that if the case went to trial it would be $500.

Following Kemp's logic, he was paying an additional $2,000 for Stringer's "political influence" to keep the case out of court.

In June 1952, the district attorney dismissed the case against Kemp because of insufficient evidence.

Kemp, unable to pay Stringer, signed two $1,000 promissory notes and then failed to make the payments. A year later, realizing he wasn't going to be able to collect, Stringer canceled the $1,000 note that had not been cosigned. He then contacted the cosigner on the second note for payment.

Kemp, angry that his cosigner had been contacted, and with his case dismissed over a year earlier, looked for a way to stop paying Herald Stringer.

He went to see assistant US Attorney Dave Talbot.

When Talbot heard Kemp's story, he'd already been involved in a couple of cases against lawyers, mostly those with drinking problems who had mishandled client funds. The charges against Herald Stringer, though, were of concern for different reasons. The amount of the fee did seem excessive, and the inference that it might pay for Stringer's "influence" was not implausible to Talbot.

Even Dave Talbot, who had been in Alaska just a couple of years, knew that Republican committeeman Herald Stringer had political clout, including being responsible for the appointment of Anchorage lawyer J. L. McCarrey Jr. to the Third Division District Court by President Dwight Eisenhower.

Whatever the motivations of the young gung-ho prosecutor, whether to prove his independence, to dispel any notion that US attorneys could be "bribed," or to take down a powerful attorney, Talbot used his "juice" and brought the case against Herald Stringer to the grand jury.

An outraged grand jury threatened to increase the charges against Stringer from unprofessional conduct to larceny by false pretenses. There was now no turning back for Dave Talbot.

Talbot, eager to move the case out of the grand jury's hands, wrote up charges on unprofessional conduct and gave the information to his boss to sign.

But US Attorney Seaborn Buckalew hesitated. Whether he didn't think the case warranted prosecution, was too politically charged, or his office was being pressured to dismiss it, the information languished on his desk.

Finally, Talbot confronted Buckalew and told him the grand jury was "hotter than a two-dollar pistol" and that if he didn't sign the information and move the Stringer case forward, the grand jury would indict Buckalew too.

Buckalew signed.

United States v. Stringer was now headed to Judge J. L. McCarrey's court.

Judge J. L. McCarrey's Conflict of Interest

Just a year earlier, when Dwight D. Eisenhower became president in 1952, Anchorage Republican committeeman and attorney Herald Stringer had searched for a suitable candidate to recommend for the Third Judicial Division post. The search wasn't easy because most of the two-dozen or so lawyers in Anchorage were Democrats.

Former Anchorage Mayor and fellow Republican John Manders seemed a likely first choice until Stringer learned of Manders' philosophical opposition to the income tax. Eventually, Stringer settled upon J. L. McCarrey Jr. A devout Mormon and family man, McCarrey had come to Alaska in the 1930s to sell stockings and clothing for the Utah Woolen Mills. He had returned to Utah to get a law degree and had been practicing law in Alaska since the 1940s.

Anchorage lawyers, though, were unimpressed with McCarrey's legal abilities. Stringer argued that it would be better to have McCarrey on the bench than an unknown appointed from another state. Heeding Stringer's advice, Anchorage lawyers endorsed McCarrey.

J. L. McCarrey Jr., US District Court judge for the Territory of Alaska. Anchorage Bar Association Oral History of Territorial Lawyers. Joint archives of the Alaska Court System and the Alaska Bar Association.

Herald Stringer, in the second row, fourth from the left, just right and behind of Grigsby, who is center of the front row. Anchorage Bar Association, Oral History of Territorial Lawyers, Pamela Cravez. Joint archives of the Alaska Court System and the Alaska Bar Association.

Now, less than a year after his appointment, with the case against Herald Stringer before him, McCarrey refused to disqualify himself. Anchorage attorneys could see that the judge intended to make an example of Herald Stringer. McCarrey would use the case to demonstrate to the public his own integrity and insistence that lawyers meet his high standards. There'd be no special favors in his court.

By the time the Stringer case came to court, Talbot had left the US attorney's office, and Juneau Assistant US Attorney James Fitzgerald took over. Fitzgerald reinterviewed the complaining witness, Kemp, and found him to be completely unreliable. He also did not find the fee excessive since attorney fees at that time were not based on hourly work. Lawyers often assessed a case and asked for a flat fee.

Fitzgerald recommended the case be dismissed.

Judge McCarrey refused.

The Anchorage bar rallied around Stringer. His defense attorneys, including Wendell Kay and George Grigsby, called fellow lawyers to testify that the fee Stringer charged was consistent with fees charged by others for "white slavery cases."

And Dave Talbot? Since he'd left the US attorney's office and gone into private practice he was beginning to feel that he had been too hasty in his judgment about the Stringer case.

In a convoluted turn of events during Stringer's trial, Talbot waffled back and forth about how the information against Stringer came to be signed. He first testified that he never threatened Buckalew with indictment if he didn't sign. And then later recanted, admitting that he had made the threats, which meant that Buckalew had been coerced into filing the case.

Whatever the truth, underlying politics, and interplay among the private bar, US attorney's office, and district court, the case record makes it very clear that Judge McCarrey put little store in the testimony of the many lawyers who came to Stringer's defense, and that the judge was determined to rule against a lawyer in a case where he had a clear conflict of interest.

Although he found no evidence of bribery or influence peddling, McCarrey did find the fee excessive. Declaring that his judicial duty "must transcend all personal emotion and human desires," he slapped Stringer with an onerous 120-day suspension from the practice of law.

Totally Unsuited to the Bench

All during the *Stringer* trial newspaper headlines ballyhooed the proceedings. Judge McCarrey's commitment to providing a judicial system free of influence peddling and overreaching by lawyers was applauded by the Anchorage community. By the time McCarrey's decision was reversed by a higher court, Stringer's reputation was damaged and his legal partnership dissolved.

Although Judge McCarrey strode into the court with his black robes, the first to look like a real judge on the Anchorage bench, lawyers found him incompetent. The Stringer case, where he should have taken himself off the case because of his conflict of interest—as the appeals court ruled—was just one example.

Under McCarrey, the court's backlog grew, delaying even minor cases for five years. When a case got before the judge, results were uncertain.

"Eventually, there were two factions formed," said defense lawyer Edgar Paul Boyko. Those who found Judge McCarrey completely incompetent did their best to resolve cases short of court. Others, like Boyko, took a more sporting view. "'Hey, we've got an obligation to our client. It's true you can't practice law in front of McCarrey, but you certainly can use child psychology.' And I did. And I kept winning cases."

Roger Cremo, who in later years developed a specialty in banking law and represented the First National Bank of Anchorage, found McCarrey "utterly unsuited" to the bench. Although McCarrey knew Cremo's opinion, the judge went out of his way to see that he did well. "I couldn't lose," Cremo said. Even when a jury came back with a verdict against Cremo's client, the judge turned it around with a judgment notwithstanding the verdict. "He bent over backwards. He was trying to show the world that he did not resent my opposition."

There wasn't much lawyers could do about Judge McCarrey's rulings from the bench or his administration of the court system. They could, however, take the power to discipline lawyers away from him.

The *Stringer* case, high profile and with devastating consequences, was just one of a number of cases throughout the territory in which lawyers questioned a district court judge's motives to discipline an attorney. In Alaska, with its small population and close dealings, lines between the personal, political, and professional were easily crossed.

Taking Power Away from the Court

In 1955, during the first territorial legislative session after the *Stringer* case, Wendell Kay, one of Stringer's attorneys and Speaker of the House, introduced a bill giving territorial lawyers the power to investigate and discipline themselves through a territorial bar association. The bill creating the Alaska Integrated Bar passed in 1955. Not surprising, since more than half of the territorial legislature were lawyers.

Under the new act, disciplinary charges against lawyers no longer went to the US attorney's office or the grand jury. They went to the territorial bar for investigation and action. The new act left only two avenues for district court involvement. The court could issue an order backing up the recommendations of the bar association's board of governors or take an appeal from a lawyer who disputed a decision of the board of governors.

Formation of the new Alaska Territorial Bar Association did much to set up a more formal hierarchy among Alaska's lawyers. A nine-member board of governors, chosen equally from around the territory, would establish the rules governing the profession. Leadership in the association fell to senior members of the bar—all but one had come to Alaska prior to 1950.

Most importantly, though, Alaska's territorial lawyers were positioning themselves for the coming of statehood. Just as the Integrated Bar was established in 1955, so too did the Constitutional Convention of 1955 provide the framework for a state judiciary.

1950s Activism on the Heels of Judicial Overreach

Judge McCarrey's decision to make an example of Herald Stringer while articulating a higher standard of justice, and Judge Folta's undercutting of US Attorney Patrick Gilmore while clamping down on prostitution and gambling in Ketchikan were just two examples of judges concerned with maintaining political and public support at the expense both of the law and the lawyers who practiced before them. There were more.

Many of the territory's private practitioners, better trained, more articulate, and with more at stake as they strived to represent their clients' interests, began to take action to limit judicial authority.

Caught in between were lawyers in the US attorneys' offices. These attorneys, members of fraternal local bars, also served the court. Young and relatively inexperienced, they found themselves in a complicated

Alaska Bar Association's first Board of Governors. *Seated left to right:* John Connolly (Anchorage), Norman Banfield (Juneau), Wilfred C. Stump (Ketchikan), Edward V. Davis (Anchorage). *Standing left to right:* Wendell Kay (Anchorage), James von der Heydt (Juneau), Charles Clasby (Fairbanks), Mike Monagle (Juneau), Julian Hurley (Fairbanks). Joint archives of the Alaska State Court and Anchorage Bar Association.

political game in which they were willing or unwilling pawns. Those US attorneys who stayed on in Alaska were usually forced to choose their allegiance. Some such as Talbot, who started as government men, mellowed considerably and blended into private practice. Others became law-and-order judges, like the judges they had served.

Still others, like Buckalew and Fitzgerald, learned a great deal from the early battles between bench and bar and went on to judicial careers of their own, sensitive to the power of both the judiciary and the bar.

Skirmishes throughout the 1950s among private practitioners, judges, and prosecutors paved the way for an unprecedented lawyer activism. The Integrated Bar Act, passed at the behest of lawyer-legislators, took the disciplinary authority away from government lawyers. No longer would the court and youthful prosecutors have the unfettered ability to destroy an attorney's reputation and business.

As statehood approached and the Constitutional Convention convened, attorneys used firsthand experience of the deficits of the territorial judiciary to support the framework for a vastly improved state judiciary. What they couldn't foresee, though, was the price they'd pay in their own professional freedom.

Lieutenant Commander Buell Nesbett during World War II. Courtesy Walt Nesbett.

Buell Nesbett: Navigating Territorial WATERS

In his later years, Buell Nesbett came to Alaska once a year from his home in Solana Beach, California, usually to go salmon fishing along the Kuskokwim River and to visit grandchildren. In 1983, the seventy-three-year-old Nesbett was a stocky man of average height, dressed Southern California style with a cardigan over a blue-and-white cotton shirt and a red tank T-shirt, over which tufts of gray-white hair peeked out.

In old photos Nesbett wears an eye patch—an injury from an airplane accident; he looks stern, erect, and has severe black eyebrows. After more than a half dozen operations to restructure the damaged eye socket, a false eye peers out. The operations had left the right side of Nesbett's face a little puffy, while the left side retained its lean demanding look under an arched eyebrow.

The eye patch suited Nesbett, a reminder of the political and personal battles fought from the time he arrived in Alaska in 1945, through his appointment and tenure as the first chief justice of Alaska's Supreme Court.

Turning Down Pillsbury, Madison, and Sutro

Since the age of sixteen, when he left his mother and stepfather's home, Nesbett had acted decisively and independently. He put himself through school, traveled around the world as a radio operator on board merchant ships, served as a probation and parole officer in San

Francisco, headed his University of San Francisco Law School class, and achieved the rank of full commander in the navy before any of his fellow officers. In 1945, discharged from the navy and recently divorced, he turned down a job in the prestigious San Francisco law firm of Pillsbury, Madison, and Sutro and decided instead to head for Alaska.

On his way up the coast by steamship, he stopped in Ketchikan, where attorney Lester Gore informed Nesbett that this small southeastern town had little to offer. Norman Banfield was equally discouraging concerning the Juneau law practice, so Nesbett headed for Anchorage.

The thirty-five-year-old ex-commander took an immediate liking to the city, where no elite lawyers or firms fixed the bar to one manner of practice. Although Nesbett appreciated the informality of Alaska's practice, he became impatient with some of its inefficiencies.

In his first job, clerking for John Manders, Nesbett watched carefully researched legal memos languish on Manders' desk. Manders, who was in the midst of running a losing race for territorial delegate to Congress on the Republican ticket, divided his time between politics and law. And, according to Nesbett, was not very successful at either. Clients repeatedly came to Manders' law office asking for their deeds and other legal forms. To Nesbett's surprise, clients tolerated these delays.

Anchorage, in 1945, still suffered the shortages of the war years, and people had learned to wait in line, put their names on lists, and not be too demanding. But Nesbett, having spent his time commanding in the navy, was used to neither shortages nor waiting. If he had to wait two or three years for a second-hand car because all auto production had gone to the war effort and the civilian business had been slow to start up, he would do so, grudgingly. But other inefficiencies of territorial Alaska could be remedied with some enterprising effort.

"That's Not the Way It's to Be Done"

Nesbett, preparing to take the written bar exam, heard tales from other members of the Anchorage bar about how long it could take from the time of the exam to receiving results and admission to practice law. The worst horror story was from those who had taken the exam in 1940, when bar examiners forgot to include a maritime question and held up admittance for two years until each of the applicants had passed a new exam with the question. Even without that glitch, Nesbett foresaw months of waiting while the exam went from one examiner to the next for grading, waiting on each of their desks for review before being sent off to the next examiner.

"That's not the way it's to be done," Nesbett said. He called territorial Attorney General Ralph Rivers and proposed making four copies of the exam, one for each examiner. Rivers agreed. Then Nesbett had Manders write to the examiners—all fellow Republicans of Manders'—urging them to quickly attend to Nesbett's test, since he was greatly needed in Manders' office.

After passing the bar exam, Nesbett didn't spend much time with Manders, finding it hard to abide his untidy work habits. Locating office space, he opened his own practice and did his own secretarial work. He remembered charging three to five dollars for a will and from two to three dollars for a deed.

He also took on overflow work from Stanley McCutcheon, who practiced in the same building as Nesbett. McCutcheon, active in Democratic politics, the territorial legislature, and a friend of Alaska Governor Ernest Gruening, welcomed Nesbett's help. The two soon became partners and stayed as such for eleven years.

Partnering with Politico Stanley McCutcheon

Stanley "Stan" McCutcheon, although several years Nesbett's junior, was a young dynamo, well educated in the political and legal affairs of the territory. Born in Anchorage in 1917, his father, Herbert Hazard "H. H." McCutcheon, a yard foreman for the Alaska Railroad, had come in the early 1900s. H. H. set the pace for Stanley and his two brothers' political futures, starting on the Anchorage city council and rising to the territorial senate. For a short time, Stanley, his older brother Steve, and H. H. all served together in the legislature.

Never taking the time to go to college, Stan McCutcheon studied with George Grigsby and Karl Drager, Anchorage's well-known trial attorneys, and was admitted to the Alaska territorial bar in 1940 on motion rather than examination.

Worrying about Precision

Even though McCutcheon was more interested in politics than law, he was good at both. His political popularity and ties to the Anchorage community brought important cases to the firm and aided in their disposition.

Stan McCutcheon on a fishing trip with Buell Nesbett. Courtesy Walt Nesbett.

McCutcheon knew all the old-timers called for jury duty. He knew how they thought and appealed to them in language they understood. Civil cases didn't interest McCutcheon, so the firm handled mostly criminal cases.

Nesbett did the research and McCutcheon performed in court. Although Nesbett worried about precision and accuracy, he noticed many of the other attorneys in town didn't share his concern.

While his partner was off in the legislature and hobnobbing with the governor, Nesbett got to know the dozen or so lawyers practicing in Anchorage. He quickly gauged the best: Ed Davis, the paper man, and Bill Renfrew, the litigator. Nesbett came up against Renfrew in court and found him rough, tough, loud, and intimidating. But also beatable.

After Nesbett beat Renfrew a few times, the two developed a rapport; they'd walk out of the courtroom, have a drink, and talk about hunting and fishing, two passions they shared. Renfrew provided Nesbett a third passion, flying. What better way to get to remote hunting and fishing spots?

Nesbett was easily persuaded to buy an airplane, the first of many, in a tumultuous flying career that ended in 1971 with the serious plane crash that left him blinded in one eye, with a fused left ankle, and with little mobility in his right forearm.

Flying, fishing, and hunting were a big part of many lawyers' lives, including Nesbett's. Courtesy Walt Nesbett.

John Rader, the state of Alaska's first attorney general, on a hunting trip with Nesbett. Courtesy Walt Nesbett.

Gordon Hartlieb, lawyer, banker, and philanthropist, at Sucker Lake with Nesbett. Courtesy Walt Nesbett.

By the time Nesbett and McCutcheon paired, law school graduates were beginning to influence a bar that had depended more upon rhetoric, bombast, and fast thinking than legal accuracy. The joining of Nesbett and McCutcheon was followed by the pairing of Warren Cuddy and Wendell Kay.

"It was the first time Warren had someone who knew how to try a case," Nesbett remembered. He added that Kay was always a gentleman in the courtroom and never needed to employ histrionics to get his point across.

But there were few demands on even well-trained lawyers like Nesbett and Kay. It was easy to slip into a practice less precise and a manner less formal. Like many of their predecessors, the new lawyers found practicing law was not a full-time occupation.

Although most of the young lawyers had not planned on alternative careers, they found themselves drafted into positions of political leadership and enjoyed it. With a flair for speaking, an ability to advocate an issue, and a working knowledge of compromise and settlement, lawyers became Anchorage's political representatives.

Nesbett served in the territorial legislature during the 1950s when half the legislature was made up of lawyers. The most visible lawyer in politics during the 1940s and early 1950s, though, was Stanley McCutcheon: Speaker of the House in 1949, House floor leader in 1951, and Democratic National Committeeman. As partner to McCutcheon, Nesbett had a front-row seat to the power and pitfalls of the territorial politics leading to statehood.

Carrying Governor Gruening's Water

In December 1939, President Franklin Roosevelt appointed Ernest Gruening governor of Alaska. Governor Gruening would serve through the war years that brought Alaska back into the public consciousness, and would lead the charge to make the territory a state. An outsider from New York, the medical-school-trained newspaperman Gruening needed allies like Stanley McCutcheon to persuade Alaskans that statehood was in their best interests. And McCutcheon obliged.

Throughout the 1940s and early 1950s McCutcheon's energy went toward pushing the governor's agenda: proposing laws to abolish the fish traps the salmon industry used to corner the fishing industry, and advocating taxes on salmon, timber, and mining interests to provide Alaska with revenue to run itself.

Outside industry opposed all attempts to encroach upon its Alaskan fiefdom, tying up any legislative successes in court challenges and delays. McCutcheon's battles, although spirited and supported by a great many resident Alaskans, would not show any gains for years. But McCutcheon was a great advocate, and even if he couldn't win in the legislature he could win in the fight for public opinion.

"He had a speech against salmon fish traps. I heard him do it at least thirty times," remembered Cliff Groh Sr., who came to practice law in

Alaska in the 1950s and partnered with McCutcheon in the 1960s. "He made me cry each time he gave it. It was that good a speech."

The close relationship between McCutcheon and Governor Gruening went beyond McCutcheon's carrying water for the governor in the territorial legislature. It extended also to McCutcheon and Nesbett's law practice, providing political support, when necessary, for the firm's clients.

Nesbett remembered Governor Gruening giving testimony regarding "public convenience and necessity" to make the Civil Aeronautics Administration act more quickly to certify Alaska Airlines to fly between Alaska, Seattle, and Portland. The testimony helped both the firm's client, Alaska Airlines, and the state. Nesbett explained: "Until then, only one air carrier served Alaska, Pacific Northern Airlines. The addition of a second air carrier from the West Coast to Alaska would draw more national attention, attention that could hasten statehood."

Mixing politics and law practice did have its drawbacks. Lawyers involved in myriad activities beyond lawyering opened themselves to broader attack.

In 1952, twenty years of Democratic rule lay buried under a Republican landslide. The Alaskan legislature reflected the national mood. Wendell Kay was elected the only Democrat in the territorial House, and then by only a six-vote margin. And in 1952, Democratic committeeman McCutcheon became the object of a vendetta at once political and professional—a scandal that made a lasting impression on McCutcheon's partner, Nesbett.

Union Bank Fiasco

On November 20, 1952, a headline screamed across the front page of the *Anchorage Daily Times*, "Order Union Bank Closed; Arrest Two Local Men." The small headline underneath read, "McCutcheon, Hassman Accused of Breaking Alaska Banking Laws." So began the public saga of a private political affair that had been brewing for some time.

A few years earlier McCutcheon, Andrew Hassman, and a few associates put together the Union Bank to compete with the other two banks in town: Elmer Rasmuson's National Bank of Alaska and Warren Cuddy's First National Bank.

"The avarice of the two banks made money quite tight. Unless you were a friend of Cuddy's or Rasmuson's it was difficult to find funds," said Stanley McCutcheon's brother, Steve.

Union Bank sought to provide an alternative lending source. For several years the bank did quite well, making loans to small operations and undercutting the other two banks by charging a percent or half a percent less in interest rates, according to Nesbett. By the end of 1951, the bank had assets of over $3 million.

When cost overruns forced a building contractor to default on his payments, the Union Bank found itself in a precarious financial position as it tried to cover its loan. It would be necessary to find another bank to help cover the loan, according to Nesbett. Both Anchorage banks were out of the question, since they welcomed their new competitor's financial difficulty. Nesbett went to Seattle to find support. Seattle First agreed to go in on the loan and then, Nesbett remembered, things began to fall apart.

The Territorial Banking Board got wind of Union Bank's plight. The board called a special meeting in Anchorage and announced its intention to declare the Union Bank in violation of its loan agreement. McCutcheon argued before the board along with Nesbett, who showed them the commitment from Seattle First to cover the delinquent loan amount.

The board went into private session and announced afterward that they were going to declare the bank in default.

As in many of the territorial controversies, views differed. Nesbett was convinced that the attorney for the National Bank of Alaska swayed the Banking Board to eliminate competition from the Union Bank. But John Hughes, Banking Board member and on retainer with NBA, disputed Nesbett's charges.

"It's true enough Rasmuson paid us $50 a month as a retainer," Hughes later said. "Big deal. That's about as far as it goes," he added, dumbfounded to learn that Nesbett blamed him and NBA for Union Bank's closure.

Hughes theorized that Banking Board chairman Marshall Crutcher, a stickler for detail, probably instigated the action.

Yet another political foe of Governor Gruening's, Marcus Jensen, had been trying to instigate a grand jury investigation of the bank as well.

Nesbett was surprised and angered that Governor Gruening, also a member of the Territorial Banking Board, did not come to McCutcheon's defense.

"Stanley, as Speaker of the House, tried his best and staked his reputation on getting through programs that [Governor] Ernest [Gruening] wanted which were for the betterment of the territory. Ernest owed it to him, but he wasn't there," Nesbett said.

J. Gerald Williams, Gruening's attorney general, remembered counseling the governor to avoid becoming involved in the Union Bank affair. Gruening called McCutcheon into his office and had Williams explain that the governor had political responsibilities that he could not risk in defense of McCutcheon.

After the Banking Board found a violation of banking laws, the matter was put into the hands of Assistant US Attorney Seaborn J. Buckalew, a former associate of McCutcheon's and Nesbett's. Buckalew called a grand jury to hear the evidence, and the panel returned a seven-count misdemeanor indictment.

The damage to the bank's reputation was irreparable, and it fell into receivership. But not for long. It still had quite a few good loans and was the third largest in the city. McCutcheon went to Dan Cuddy, and Cuddy, within four days of the initial closure, reopened the bank under his ownership.

McCutcheon resigned from his position with the bank. As for the misdemeanor charges returned by the grand jury, Nesbett researched every point and each count was dismissed for failure to state a violation of the law.

McCutcheon Bounces Back

The day after the Union Bank was sold to Cuddy, McCutcheon made the front page of Anchorage's newspaper for successfully defending a woman accused of killing her common law husband. The jury acquitted the woman over prosecutor Buckalew's protest.

McCutcheon's closing argument typified the trial lawyer's courtroom flourish. McCutcheon characterized the man his client was accused of killing as a "beast," a "Frankenstein," an "overgrown Gigolo," and a "Great Big Hero of the North." "What kind of man would it be that would make such a promise [of marriage] to a girl and then sponge off of her and beat her?" This death was not the woman's fault, but that of the highway patrol who failed to heed her cries for help when she reported a beating the night before.

After the Union Bank episode, McCutcheon and Nesbett put aside Gruening's desertion and continued to work with, and for, the governor.

McCutcheon remained the consummate politician and public figure, proposing debates between Democrat and Republican candidates, trying cases, and running for public office. However, less than a year later, Gruening was replaced by President Eisenhower's appointment of a new Republican governor for Alaska, B. Frank Heintzleman, and Stanley McCutcheon's political power waned.

Nesbett Battens Down the Hatches

Even thirty years later, Nesbett still felt the sting of Governor Gruening's desertion and having his work to save the bank dispensed with. "It was total politics," Nesbett said.

The Union Bank episode counted as only one in a series of Republican attempts to discredit McCutcheon. Others included numerous IRS audits and a fruitless congressional investigation of McCutcheon for possible communist leanings during the McCarthy era.

Partnering with McCutcheon throughout this period of political backlash took its toll on Nesbett. Researching claims, supporting his partner, and presenting what he considered solid legal cases that were dispensed with out of political and financial expediency wore Nesbett down. He remembered these days as his heaviest drinking days.

"If you worked hard on a case, you'd drive yourself and have a tendency to have a drink and work harder," he said. "Pretty soon you get to depending on it. [I] got to trying lots of cases and working and drinking [hard]. I finally reached a point where I said, 'Hell, this is no life for me. I got to quit it.' So I did."

Nesbett tackled drinking with the same single-mindedness that he tackled everything. In 1953, the same year that Governor Gruening left office, Nesbett went dry, determined to cut alcohol out of his life. People recall seeing a transformation in his personality. He was no longer so mellow or easygoing.

Although in McCutcheon's shadow politically, Nesbett's partnership gave him a good vantage point from which to assess the territory's progress toward statehood—and its ramifications for those like McCutcheon who worked to capitalize on the political, legal, and commercial opportunities. Nesbett understood the players, the politics, and the stakes.

In the coming years, Nesbett would use this knowledge not as a territorial legislator or delegate to the Constitutional Convention, but as a leader in the Anchorage bar. It would be among Anchorage's private practitioners that he'd work to influence the framework for a state judiciary and the selection of those who would serve on the first courts.

13 ★

Anchorage Lawyers: Creating a BETTER SYSTEM

The Anchorage bar grew and changed as well-educated and ambitious young lawyers looked to Alaska for opportunity and adventure in the 1950s. To these lawyers, the novelty of the territorial system outweighed its idiosyncrasies and inefficiencies. They built their careers as the last battles between territorial lawyers and judges wore on. Statehood would propel many of these young lawyers into positions of power and influence. But it would be the decade prior to statehood where their ambition and innovation as lawyers would first shine.

Hartlieb, Groh, and Rader: Road Map for Success

Gordon Hartlieb, a graduate of Kent State Law School, was appointed US commissioner in Anchorage in 1954. Clifford Groh Sr. received his law degree from the University of New Mexico Law School and began work in Anchorage as assistant US attorney in 1953. John Rader, who served as Anchorage city attorney in 1954, came to Alaska in 1951 after graduating from the University of Kansas Law School. In 1955, the three established the Anchorage law firm, Hartlieb, Groh, and Rader.

Each individually would go on to have a lasting impact upon the state of Alaska.

Hartlieb would leave his mark as a banker, labor consultant, member of the Anchorage City Council, and supporter of legal, business, and vocational education at the University of Alaska–Anchorage.

Cliff Groh in the 1960s. Courtesy Groh family.

Groh would become president of Operation Statehood in 1953 and spend a lifetime in public service, including service in the state legislature, borough assembly, Anchorage School Board, and Anchorage Charter Commission.

John Rader, an active Democrat and champion of individual rights, would become Alaska's first attorney general—handling the state's legal affairs including abolition of fish traps, spending more than ten years in the Alaska legislature, and being instrumental in establishing the administrative framework for the state.

In 1955, though, these three joined to a build a firm that would lay the foundation for their future success, service, and philanthropy. They developed a legal practice focused on work that did not depend upon the territorial court. Elmer Rasmuson hired the firm to be chief counsel for the National Bank of Alaska. The unions hired the firm after the unions' lawyer was disbarred due to a drinking habit. And a portion of their real estate work came after another territorial lawyer retired.

Although they worked hard for their clients, they realized that practicing law was not a big moneymaker. A client would come in and ask for advice on a piece of property. The three would confer and give an answer. The client would make a lot of money. The lawyers would make $25 an hour.

They came to an arrangement that would change this. Every month each took $1,000 out of the firm account and invested it for the firm. Any money that went out of the firm had to be okayed by more than one partner, and any investment made by any of the lawyers, even aside from the regular $1,000, had to be made jointly for the entire firm.

The result: the first year Gordon Hartlieb worked for the firm he made $17,000 compared to the $7,500 he made the year before as commissioner.

The firm did well and so did its clients. After statehood, passage of a branch-banking bill paved the way for NBA to have a statewide presence. Rader was attorney general at the time. But as Groh and Rader became more and more active in politics, the bulk of the daily legal work fell to Hartlieb. Hiring associates didn't make up for the lack of partner participation, and the three decided to dissolve their partnership. They split among them assets acquired over ten years that included Homestate Insurance Company of Alaska, Security Title (which they sold for $1.6 million in 1980), and First Federal Savings and Loan (for which Gordon Hartlieb served as chairman for thirty years).

Nesbett Leads Anchorage Bar toward Statehood

While lawyers like Hartlieb, Groh, and Rader developed practices that depended less upon the courts, it was not possible for most other lawyers.

Fights between the bar and bench spilled over into the newspaper. Lawyer-legislator Warren Taylor, incensed by Judge Folta's lobbying of the legislature for laws he believed would unfairly impact criminal defendants, accused the judge of being a "hanging judge." Judge Folta responded to Taylor, calling the defense attorney more interested in his criminal clientele's welfare than that of the general public.

Lawyer-legislators Wendell Kay, Warren Taylor, Tom Stewart, and others supported legislation creating the Integrated Bar, giving lawyers the right to manage their own profession and handle their own disciplinary matters. Territorial legislators, including Stewart, called for a Constitutional Convention in 1955 to develop, among other things, the framework for a state judiciary.

Newer members of the bar watched long-simmering animosities being played out in the court of public opinion and in the territorial legislature. They understood the confrontational nature of the profession and also understood the need for a way forward.

Along with older office practitioners like John Hughes, Raymond Plummer, and George Hayes, young private practitioners pushed for bar leadership they could trust to advocate for their profession and a modern state judiciary. They sought a person who understood territorial politics and players. Someone whose legal ability they respected. Someone with integrity and independence. And, most importantly, someone passionate about taking part in creating the best court system possible for Alaska.

They found this person in Buell Nesbett.

The push for Nesbett to head the Anchorage bar had one drawback. It meant dislodging septuagenarian George Grigsby from his "president for life" position.

The gold rush attorney Grigsby had taken little interest in the events that were shaping future law practice. While some lawyers encouraged the more activist-oriented Nesbett to run against Grigsby, Nesbett remembered also being approached by "the other side."

A group of older attorneys asked Nesbett not to throw Grigsby out of office. It was agreed that if Nesbett accepted the title of vice president he could act as president. The group then arranged for Grigsby to continue as president "emeritus" of the Anchorage bar.

Nesbett took the helm of the Anchorage bar knowing that he would need to attend to the old faction that loved a good fight and crafty legal maneuvering. Although he'd partnered with McCutcheon for years, who had some of this in him, Nesbett never counted himself among this group.

"Frankly, I was never, to put it bluntly, in the same boat with Wendell [Kay] or with any of those fellas . . . I always held back because I didn't approve of some of the things they'd laugh about and do in their practice and the way they'd handle things and the way they did politics," he said, looking back.

He stayed away from them. He could tell they resented his distance. He also understood that Kay resented that lawyers had come to Nesbett to be president, not him.

"But the fellas came to me," Nesbett said.

Still, when Kay would go on a bender, Kay's secretary would come to Nesbett's office at the First National Bank. "He's due in court at 10 and it's 9:30," Nesbett remembered her telling him and handing over Kay's files. "I'd always go in and handle his cases for him and take care of it."

Judiciary committee meeting at the Constitutional Convention. *Left to right:* Irwin Metcalf, R. E. Robertson, Maurice Johnson, George McLaughlin (chair), Sheldon Elliott (consultant), Ralph Rivers, Thomas Harris, and Ed Davis (Anchorage lawyer meeting with committee). Joint archives of the Alaska Court System and the Alaska Bar Association.

What Will the State Judiciary Look Like?

In 1955, the territory convened a Constitutional Convention in Fairbanks to provide a framework of laws for the future state. There were fifty-five delegates to the convention, thirteen of whom were lawyers.

Nesbett was not a member of the convention. Still, he received daily reports from the judiciary committee and made his opinions known. Lawyers dominated the judiciary committee at the convention, with Anchorage attorney and former municipal judge George McLaughlin chairing. Juneau lawyer R. E. Robertson, Fairbanks lawyer Warren Taylor, former territorial attorney general Ralph Rivers, and Fairbanks attorney Maurice Johnson also served on the committee, with Valdez hotel manager and chamber of commerce president Thomas Harris and Seward merchant and former US marshal Irwin Metcalf.

The minutes of the Constitutional Convention reflect some of the concerns that lawyers had regarding political appointments and elected judges. If unilaterally appointed by the governor, judges could be controlled by a political machine; if elected, they could be indebted to financial backers needed in every election.

Tom Stewart, who after statehood would be appointed to the Superior Court, served as executive director of the Statehood Committee and secretary of the Constitutional Convention. Prior to the convening of delegates, Stewart worked with consultants who developed briefing papers on major topics for the convention, providing delegates with the latest policy research on constitutional topics. The briefing paper on the judicial article recommended simplicity so that changes could be made as the state grew, that Alaska have a "unified" court system administered centrally rather than by individual communities, and that judges be appointed by the governor from candidates screened by a nonpartisan body of lawyers and citizens similar to that in the "Missouri Plan."

Much of the substance of these recommendations was adopted, according to Alaska Supreme Court Justice Warren W. Matthews (Ret.) at the fiftieth anniversary of the Constitutional Convention in 2005. He recalled that Juneau lawyer and Judiciary Committee member Robertson submitted his own proposal for the judiciary article to fellow committee members. Robertson's version included the provision that the Alaska Bar Association be the body to recommend attorneys to the governor for appointment rather than a judicial council of lawyers and laypersons. This recommendation, which would have given lawyers sole authority to recommend judicial appointees, was not adopted. Instead, the committee recommended adoption of the Missouri Plan.

The plan called for a merit system wherein the governor would appoint candidates nominated by a citizens' commission called the Judicial Council. This system dictated that practicing lawyers would evaluate their fellow lawyers under consideration for judicial posts. A judicial council, made up of six voting members, three lawyers, and three laypersons, along with the chief justice of the Alaska Supreme Court who would vote in case of a tie, would rely upon the evaluations and provide the governor with a pool from which to select appointees.

The Alaska Bar Association would appoint the three lawyer-members to the judicial council. The governor would appoint the lay members. Judges would be subject to mandatory retention elections every three years and then every subsequent decade.

This system provided the bar association input in selecting judicial candidates, something it had little of during territorial years, but not sole control.

The judicial article provided an outline, but many details would need to be filled in before the Alaska state judicial system could function. Bar members throughout the state began working on providing recommendations.

In Fairbanks, Charles Clasby drafted a judicial code and asked the local bar to comment. Under Nesbett's leadership, the Anchorage Bar Association set up committees on judicial reorganization: Inferior Courts, Judicial Salaries, Retirement, Budget, Jurisdictions, and Venue. The notion that lawyers could provide recommendations to organize the system under which they would practice was a heady tonic.

When Congress passed the Alaska Statehood Act in 1958, lawyers saw an end to years of an inept and inefficient territorial judicial system and the opportunity to make recommendations for the first slate of Alaska state judges.

Who Would Become Judge?

In anticipation of a new state judiciary, the Alaska bar began the process of selecting the three lawyers to represent their views on the judicial council.

Each of the three major Alaska judicial divisions—Anchorage, Fairbanks, and Southeast—was to have a member on the judicial council. The constitution was silent, however, on the question of how the Alaska Bar Association was to choose these lawyers.

In Anchorage, Nesbett, along with Edward Davis, Ralph Cottis, and James Fitzgerald, proposed a democratic system involving nominations, ballots, and votes, with provisions for a runoff in case of no clear majority.

Juneau's Frank Doogan suggested to the Anchorage Bar Association that local bar associations establish a statewide system for selecting judicial council members. However, before the local bars could come to an agreement, the Alaska Bar Association's board of governors made their own decision.

In 1959, the board of governors met in Nome and "acted in a way that had never been anticipated," said retired Superior Court Judge Tom Stewart, who had helped draft both the constitution and the Integrated Bar Act.

The board's appointments to the state's first judicial council would have packed the court system with judges sympathetic to plaintiffs. The

Alaska's first superior and supreme court judges. Seated left to right: Justices Walter Hodge, Buell A. Nesbett, and John H. Dimond. Standing left to right: Superior Court Judges Walter E. Walsh, Harry O. Arend; J. Earl Cooper; Everett W. Hepp, Hubert A. Gilbert, James A. von der Heydt, Edward V. Davis and James M. Fitzgerald. November 27, 1959, swearing-in ceremony of first state superior court judges, Juneau. Joint archives of the Alaska Court System and the Alaska Bar Association.

selections made in Nome provided that Ernie Bailey of Ketchikan, Robert Parrish of Fairbanks, and Herald Stringer of Anchorage would serve as the lawyer-members of the judicial council.

These lawyers—two of whom had extensive plaintiff-oriented practices and the third of whom was friendly with the bar's personal injury faction—would have easily overpowered the judicial council's three lay members with block votes. They would have presented the governor with a group of ideologically identical judicial candidates.

But for some very unhappy board members and some outraged lawyers in Anchorage—including Nesbett—the board of governors would have gotten away with this power grab.

Edward Davis presided over a meeting of the Anchorage bar at the Loussac Library in downtown Anchorage. Angry lawyers threatened to convene a special meeting to recall the board of governors if the board did not withdraw the judicial council candidates.

Nesbett and James Fitzgerald were dispatched to talk to Herald Stringer, the Anchorage candidate for the judicial council. Stringer agreed to take himself out of the running provided that his former partner and board of governor member John Connolly not be censured for his part in the attempt to pack the first courts.

The Anchorage bar voted to submit Nesbett's and Raymond Plummer's names to the board of governors to replace Stringer. Although there was some effort in Fairbanks and Southeast to switch judicial council candidates, only the Anchorage candidate was changed.

Raymond Plummer joined Ernie Bailey and Robert Parrish as the third lawyer-member of the judicial council. This addition paved the way for the two who had protested the original lawyer makeup of the council to become judges: Edward Davis to be appointed Superior Court judge in Anchorage and Buell Nesbett to become the first chief justice of the Alaska Supreme Court.

Nesbett took his seat on the Alaska Supreme Court along with fellow justices, John Dimond (the son of former US District Court Judge Anthony Dimond), and Walter Hodge. Hodge left to become US Federal District Court judge and was replaced by Harry O. Arend from Fairbanks in 1960.

During his first year as chief justice, Nesbett's command of administrative tasks impressed everyone. He organized the state court system, implemented a system of using tape recorders rather than stenographers in the courtroom—a novel concept at the time that would save money—and headquartered the Supreme Court in Anchorage, rather than Juneau, the state capital.

His ideas had some opposition, but as fellow Justice John Dimond observed, "He was commander of a destroyer during the war [and] he had some of that concept of authority as chief justice."

Nesbett's move to chief justice from "president" of the Anchorage bar heralded the coming of a judicial system more professional, expert, and forward thinking.

The Integrated Bar Act gave private practitioners power over their profession. Adoption of the Missouri Plan and establishment of the Judicial Council provided lawyers, who knew one another well, the opportunity to evaluate candidates for appointment to the bench. It also gave lawyers a vote on who would be appointed.

With many of the power struggles of the 1950s behind them and statehood a reality, the horizon seemed clear for smooth sailing.

However, as Nesbett took steps to fortify Alaska's judicial system, lawyers began to feel the power they'd been assured threatened.

The fights prior to statehood between bench and bar would be small compared to the one to come.

Alaska Superior Court judges on their way to judicial training in New Jersey. Joint archives of the Alaska Court System and the Alaska Bar Association.

14 ★
Rocky SEAS: The Great ALASKA Court-Bar FIGHT

Clyde Houston made a pact with himself when he was sixteen years old that he would never make a move without knowing where his next paycheck was coming from. Growing up in a family that struggled during the Depression, Houston graduated high school in 1941 and moved to Seattle looking for work to support himself. But at sixteen he was too young to work legally and too broke to turn back. He lied about his age and got a job peeling timber for pilings at the Port of Seattle. The experience made him careful. In 1960, the thirty-six-year-old Houston was practicing law in Warden, Washington, and heard the new state of Alaska needed lawyers. So much so that experienced lawyers could get a job in the state attorney general's office without having to take the Alaska bar exam.

No lawyer enjoys taking the bar exam, especially an exam in a new state with unfamiliar case law. Who knew what the questions would be and how the test would be graded? When your livelihood depends upon passing the bar exam, the stakes are high.

Houston, who had been practicing for seven years, had no problem being hired for a job in the Juneau attorney general's office and moved his family there in 1960. After a year he transferred to Anchorage as a prosecutor for the state, appearing in court frequently, still with no need for an Alaska license. Tiring of trial work with the state, Houston made plans to go into private practice and contacted the Alaska Bar Association in October 1961 to be admitted to the Alaska bar. He'd been practicing for nearly a decade and didn't think there would be any trouble with his being admitted on "reciprocity," since he'd already been admitted in Washington State.

The only problem was that Washington State did not admit Alaskans on "reciprocity"—meaning that if an Alaskan wanted to practice in Washington State they would be required to take the Washington State bar exam. The Alaska bar refused to admit Houston, letting him know that he would have to take the Alaska bar exam if he wanted to go into private practice.

Houston asked the board of governors to reconsider.

They remained adamant, although they did let Houston know he could take a special lawyers' examination rather than the full exam. Angered by the bar association's demand, Houston appealed to the Alaska Supreme Court to grant his admission to practice.

What could have remained a narrow disagreement over whether a Washington lawyer had the right to be admitted on reciprocity to the Alaska bar became, instead, the spark that ignited a great power struggle between Alaska lawyers and the Alaska Supreme Court. More particularly, a brawl between Alaska lawyers and Chief Justice Buell Nesbett that's come to be known as the "court-bar fight."

In 1963, Clyde Houston was not the only one complaining about how the Alaska bar operated and how it made its decisions.

Where Does the Alaska Bar Belong?

Alaska legislators had been getting an earful from their constituents about the bar association not doing enough to police its members. Although there'd been a rash of suspensions after statehood dealing with lawyers overcharging, absconding with funds, and providing questionable representation, in the following years suspensions slowed to a trickle.

But not in Anchorage, according to Dave Talbot. Talbot, the original assistant US attorney to bring disciplinary charges against Herald Stringer in the fated 1950s case, now led the Anchorage bar's grievance committee. Talbot had mellowed considerably. When a disciplinary matter came to his attention, he followed a discreet procedure. He would call the attorney in question, see him after work hours, and tell him about the problem. "With any luck at all, by five the next night there is no more problem," said Talbot. "You straighten it out with his

Chief Justice Buell Nesbett.
Joint archives of the Alaska
Court System and the Alaska
Bar Association.

client, with his opponent, or with the judge. You make a little note for
the file, mark it closed, and go on to something else." But, he added, in
Ketchikan and Fairbanks grievance matters could go on for years and
citizens were complaining to their elected representatives: What good
was a new state court system if there was nothing to stop dishonest
lawyers from practicing law?

Legislators took a look at the act that created the bar association in
1955 and were surprised to see that the bar was not a governmental
agency. It was not under the executive branch or the legislative or even
the judicial branch of government. It was on its own, and there were no
checks and balances built in to monitor its operations.

This didn't seem right to some legislators, so they drafted a bill to put
the bar association under the executive branch of government. Senate
Bill 61 would transform the bar's board of governors into administrative
appointees. In February 1963, lawyers from the bar association's board
of governors contacted fellow lawyer, Robert McNealy, who was also
majority leader in the Alaska Senate, and expressed their opposition
to McNealy as well as other lawyer-legislators, hoping to block the bill
from going further.

Déjà vu All Over Again

Chief Justice Nesbett, too, was hearing from irate citizens about lawyers needing to be disciplined. By 1963, he'd gained much public trust, creating the administrative framework for Alaska's Superior and Supreme Courts, presiding over Alaska's first state Supreme Court, and writing decisions with his fellow justices. Many of the Supreme Court's early decisions defined the roles and responsibilities of federal and state officials as Alaska transitioned from territory to state. The court made clear that, when necessary, federal and state officials shared authority, so that any confusion would not interfere with the prosecution of cases.

After three years of working to make the court responsive to the needs of the new state, providing oversight of lawyers who practiced before the court seemed a natural progression. As legislators considered locating the bar under the executive branch, Nesbett took Clyde Houston's appeal and staked the court's claim.

Nesbett wrote the decision admitting Clyde Houston to the practice of law in Alaska, declaring that the Supreme Court, rather than the Alaska Bar Association, had "the inherent and final power and authority to determine the standards for admission to the practice of law" in Alaska.

Territorial lawyers received the opinion with an eerie sense of déjà vu. The state judiciary they'd created was spreading its wings and grabbing hold of their practice and profession, just as the territorial district court had.

A month after issuing his decision in the *Houston* case, Chief Justice Nesbett suggested to Alaska Bar Association President Robert Ziegler that the bar association vote at its next meeting to request that the Alaska Bar Association be placed under the judiciary—a vote very unlikely to pass.

Whether the request was an attempt at transparency, a courtesy, or a warning, before lawyers had a chance to vote, the Alaska Senate passed a resolution placing the bar under the judiciary and suggesting the Supreme Court prepare rules to make this happen.

Chief Justice Nesbett quickly obliged. He put Anchorage attorney Burton Biss in charge of examining rules of bar associations around the country and drafting rules for Alaska. Biss, distancing himself from the controversy years later, remembered spending "all of a good day on it," providing Nesbett with a streamlined set of rules for governing the bar. Nesbett sent copies of the rules to lawyers around the state for comment. The Juneau bar reacted favorably, the Anchorage bar sharply against, and the board of governors reserved its opinion.

Sensing opposition, Nesbett had his administrative director of courts, Tom Stewart, take a second look at the rules. Stewart, born in Juneau, law clerk to territorial District Court Judge George Folta, statehood supporter, and secretary to the Constitutional Convention in 1955, understood the gravity and politics behind Justice Nesbett's request.

He spent time comparing various states' bar rules and determined that Biss had made the Michigan rules his primary model but excluded a crucial step relating to the disciplinary process. In Michigan, a three-judge panel from lower courts prepared initial findings, while the Supreme Court served only as an appellate body. Biss' scheme left out the special panel, making the Supreme Court the sole arbiter.

Stewart told Nesbett that the rules left the Supreme Court too involved in the disciplinary procedure. They provided for no appellate procedure. He suggested the court use the Michigan format with some minor alterations, still leaving the Supreme Court an appellate role.

Nesbett refused this advice.

"Off the Wall and Out of the Blue"

On Good Friday, March 27, 1964, the biggest earthquake to ever be recorded in North America hit south central Alaska. The magnitude 9.2 quake lasted more than four-and-a-half minutes and was followed by a stream of aftershocks. In its wake, Anchorage neighborhoods were destroyed, landslides collapsed bluffs along Cook Inlet, and the control tower at the Anchorage airport fell. Tsunamis hit Seward, Kodiak, and other cities on the coast, causing over one hundred deaths.

Downtown law offices, where the earthquake ripped across Fourth Avenue, splitting apart the road and sinking the north side of the street, lay in shambles. Lawyers were still cleaning debris and dealing with the aftermath when they received a big packet of papers with new rules from the Supreme Court on April 7.

Two weeks later, Wendell Kay, now president of the Anchorage bar, brought his copy of the new rules to the bar's weekly Monday luncheon. No one had read them. He asked Dave Talbot, head of the Anchorage bar's disciplinary committee, to review them and report back.

Talbot went home and dug out his packet and began reading. "I was horrified," Talbot said. "It was a purported takeover. . . . It abolished the statutory bar and created a new bar association as part of the Supreme Court. It was right off the wall and out of the blue."

Talbot called Kay and told him, "We're in trouble."

Calm, Cool, Positive Action

The board of governors of the Alaska bar kept a neutral public face as it watched efforts to diminish its autonomy, first by putting the Alaska Bar Association under the executive branch and next under the Supreme Court. They set up a committee to lobby and develop legislation to block the takeovers. Understanding that the situation could quickly deteriorate into something "heated and aimless," the board of governors called for "calm, cool, positive action." Alaska Bar Association President David Thorsness met with Nesbett in May to see if the rules could be modified. Thorsness reported that the chief justice met his overtures with "complete indifference."

The Alaska Bar Association voted to reject the proposed bar rules and authorized the board to disregard them if enacted. Incoming bar president Robert Ziegler appointed Wendell Kay, David Talbot, Eugene Wiles, Richard McVeigh, and George Boney to a committee in charge of retaining counsel and writing an opinion regarding the institution of a suit in federal court if the rules were put into effect.

On June 1, the Supreme Court activated the bar rules. Nesbett, the veteran attorney whom the bar had confidently endorsed in 1960 as the first Supreme Court justice, was displaying the same intractable will that had previously endeared him to the bar. Now Nesbett not only threatened the bar's independence, but also offended its sense of fairness.

Those most angered by Nesbett's actions were members of the Anchorage bar. "Nesbett wanted to be the man on the white horse after he became Chief Justice, but he hadn't been a man on a white horse up until that time and the other lawyers knew that," recalled Anchorage attorney Kenneth R. Atkinson.

To the Anchorage bar, Nesbett was beginning to look a lot like territorial district court judges who tried to use their position to tame the bar. It hadn't worked then; it wasn't going to work now.

Man on the White Horse Charges

On July 23, Justice Nesbett took over the Alaska Bar Association. He'd polled the board of governors earlier, asking whether they would serve under the Supreme Court. No one responded to his poll. Interpreting their lack of response as refusal to serve, Nesbett dismissed the board, made the Supreme Court "temporary trustee" of the bar, and ordered all of the bar's assets into the custody of the Supreme Court.

Justice Dimond, Nesbett's colleague on the court, a tall, mild mannered man whose father had been a temperate district court judge in the 1940s and 1950s, could do little to influence Nesbett's course. He registered his opposition to the poll of the board, fearing it would harden the opposition.

"When you're put in a position to make decisions like the court was, you don't run to people and ask them how to decide cases or appeals," Nesbett said, explaining his style of management as chief justice. "Administrative matters, you're supposed to know it, if you don't you better find out and study it and decide."

The same day he took over the bar, Nesbett sent administrator Tom Stewart to First National Bank of Anchorage to move the bar funds into a trust account. Stewart drew up a writ of sequestration, and at Nesbett's direction, walked down the street to the bank to serve the writ and take the bar's money.

Court Takes Bar Funds at Gunpoint

On July 23, Roger Cremo sat at his desk at the First National Bank on Fourth Avenue, just down the street from the courthouse. He'd gotten a call saying that Tom Stewart would be over after hours with a writ to take bar funds. When Stewart arrived with a trooper, Cremo came down from his office to meet them. He looked over the writ.

"I'm not sure of the legality of this and what our response should be," Cremo said to Stewart. "Do you mind if I consider it overnight?"

Stewart left the writ with Cremo for review and arranged to come back before the bank opened the next morning.

When Nesbett learned that Stewart had left without moving bar funds, he was upset.

Stewart and the trooper returned before business hours the next morning, and the cashier had the check ready for them. But before he would deliver the check, the cashier said he had to call Mr. Cremo. Stewart remembered the following: The cashier got Cremo on the phone and spoke with him. He then turned to the trooper, who was not in uniform, and asked, "Do you have a gun?" The officer shrugged and said, "Yes."

The cashier reported that the trooper had a gun. Cremo asked the cashier whether the trooper had shown the gun to him. "No," the cashier replied. "Have him show it to you." The cashier turned to the trooper, "Can I see your gun?"

The trooper opened his jacket so that the cashier could see his gun in a shoulder holster. He closed his coat. The cashier told Cremo over the phone that the officer had shown him his gun. "Has he pulled his gun?" Cremo asked. "No," the cashier responded.

"We don't think it's legal unless we're forced to. Ask him to pull his gun." The officer pulled his gun. Then Cremo asked the cashier to have the officer point the gun at Stewart, which he did with his hand outside the trigger guard.

The cashier handed over the funds and Stewart set up the trust account. Less than an hour later the *Anchorage Times* was on the street with the headline: "Court Takes Bar Funds at Gunpoint."

Although accused of setting up the court, Cremo objected, saying, "There are only two ways to get money from a bank, by force or a writ." The writ Stewart gave him was "completely invalid," Cremo said. He had no choice—the only other way to get money from a bank is by force.

Cremo didn't call the newspaper, but he did tell colleagues what happened and the call was made.

The news didn't stop with the *Anchorage Times*. When Stewart reached New York a few days later for a meeting of the National Association of Court Administrators, he found newspapers there full of the same story. "Why did the court use a gun to take bar funds?" he was asked time and again. It was difficult to explain the situation in Alaska to a New York bar.

Hammer and Tongs

Nesbett had good reason to worry when Stewart told him he'd left the writ for bar funds with Cremo to "think about" overnight. For five years, Nesbett had been president of the Anchorage Bar Association. He knew the most active members were aggressive plaintiffs' lawyers who won cases by being "rough and tough in court." You only needed about 25 percent of the bar to get anything done since the "fat cat defense lawyers that represent insurance companies were apathetic," Nesbett said. "Davis and Renfrew, which is Hughes, Thorsness, Plummer and Delany [in the 1980s, Delaney, Wiles], all those are just busy representing insurance companies at $75 an hour, they really didn't take much of an interest in the bar."

Nesbett, though, knew it would be "hammer and tongs" with the plaintiffs' attorneys.

But Nesbett misjudged the depth of opposition among lawyers to the court's actions, which by now involved more than taking over the bar association. During this time the court also began to require a bond of no more than $30 to be paid by the losing party in a civil suit to cover jury costs. The court suggested, too, that it was considering requiring copies of all contingent fee contracts between attorneys and clients to be filed with the trial court and be reviewed after judgment to determine whether the contract was fair in light of the work done. The court explained, in press releases, the public benefits. Lawyers, particularly plaintiffs' lawyers, were incensed.

"It was rough there for quite a while. But I felt that that was the right thing to do. So, if the heat was intense, that was just part of the job," Nesbett said.

Five days after seizure of the bar's bank account, the Alaska Bar Association brought suit in federal court against the Alaska Supreme Court, the individual members of the court, and the court administrator.

In response, Nesbett sent out press releases calling the case a "one-sided controversy" focused on the court making rules for the disciplining of attorneys. Press releases explained that during territorial years, lawyers weren't disciplining themselves very well because the territorial court had no oversight of disciplinary procedures. The Alaska Supreme Court rules remedied this.

Nesbett assured the public that only a small, volatile portion of the bar was behind the controversy. In reality, nearly every member of the bar paid a special assessment to fight the case. And most bar members lent their names to the official case title.

Nesbett continued to direct his attacks at the Anchorage bar, knowing their nature and believing they led the fight. Now, though, Fairbanks and Juneau lawyers had entered the fray. As Robert Ziegler of Ketchikan recalled, "We were practicing attorneys, we knew what was good for us.

We knew what was bad for us. We likewise knew what was good for the people we represented and what was bad for them. The Supreme Court in those days was icily aloof."

"Winging It"

In the days to come, each side did its best to bolster its position and keep the other off balance. Nesbett, upon learning that disciplinary committees around the state were, under protest, complying with the rules and clearing disciplinary cases, rescinded the Supreme Court order making the court trustee of the bar. The court prepared to return the bar's funds and files, but the bar's board of governors had no interest in operating under the authority of the court and refused to take the files and funds back. Both sides understood, too, that with the return of files and funds the Supreme Court's actions would appear less egregious to the federal court.

The bar enlisted the aid of Joseph Ball, a prominent California lawyer who had just been to Alaska for a bar convention and so impressed the membership that it asked him to be their counsel. In a purposefully haphazard fashion, the bar allowed counsel to set its strategy, and only a few were informed of the direction. Bar secretary Atkinson remembered feeling like a pawn, getting no absolute instructions and ending up "sort of winging it." As he recalled, "They were letting everybody improvise what they were going to do to see how it came out and if something happened that was to the advantage of the lawyers that's fine." The strategy would make it more difficult for the court to deal in any concrete way with the membership.

The court, though, had its own strategy to strengthen its position prior to meeting the Alaska Bar Association in federal district court.

While it continued to appeal to the public through press releases, it also accepted a new case that would provide an opportunity to rule on its power to set all bar rules.

The decision in Clyde Houston's case gave the court the power to admit attorneys. Now, the court looked for another case to show it had the power to make all rules for the bar, not just rules for admission.

Nesbett went along with a scheme devised by his attorney, George Cochran Doub. Anchorage attorney Harland W. Davis was asked to petition the court to decide whether it had the power to make rules for governing the bar association.

When lawyers saw Davis' petition to the court, they became suspicious and deposed him. Davis quickly admitted that he'd petitioned the court at Nesbett's instigation and agreed to withdraw his petition. But Nesbett and the court refused to let Davis withdraw his petition, although allowing the case to proceed made the court vulnerable to charges of procuring cases to enhance its own power.

In the meantime, making clear its intent to handle disciplinary cases more expeditiously than the bar and demonstrating its prerogative to be notified of all disciplinary matters whether or not the bar was acting upon them, the Supreme Court reopened a disciplinary case. Neil Mackay, an Anchorage attorney, had been accused of overcharging a client in the 1950s and had been exonerated by the board of governors.

The consequences of Nesbett's decision to reopen a closed case against Neil Mackay reached, according to some, far beyond the confines of the court-bar fight, though even here they were significant and long lasting. Perhaps Nesbett felt justified looking into this case. Perhaps he knew, even then, that something was not quite right. Whether his actions against Mackay set in motion the controversies to come is certainly debatable. What isn't, is that opening this case changed the course of the court-bar fight and forever altered the Alaska Supreme Court.

Alaska Supreme Court Justice Harry Arend, Chief Justice Buell Nesbett, and Justice John Dimond. Joint archives of the Alaska Court System and the Alaska Bar Association.

15 ★
Nesbett's Surrogate

When he served as president of the Anchorage bar in the 1950s, Buell Nesbett received a complaint against lawyer Neil Mackay for taking advantage of a real estate client. Mackay, had, like Nesbett, come to Alaska after spending time in the navy during World War II. Instead of spending the war at sea, Mackay had spent it in the air as a marine pilot and flight instructor. After the war he went to law school and arrived in Anchorage in 1951 at the age of twenty-eight. Before being admitted to the bar, Mackay worked as a vice president for the First National Bank of Alaska and became familiar with the Anchorage real estate market. According to journalist Tom Brennan, Mackay used insider knowledge of foreclosures and individuals in financial distress to acquire land and buildings at "bargain prices." After passing the bar in 1954, Mackay left the bank and opened two businesses in one building on Fourth Avenue: a mortuary in front and a law office in the back. Mackay also continued to invest in real estate, and by the end of the 1950s, was a very wealthy man.

When Nesbett received the complaint against Mackay in the 1950s, he referred the matter to David Thorsness, chairman of the Alaska bar's grievance committee. That was the last he'd heard of it.

Now, in the middle of the court-bar fight, Nesbett found the disciplinary case against Neil Mackay among the bar files the Supreme Court had taken. Nesbett read the case. A committee of the bar initially voted 2–1 to discipline Mackay. Mackay appealed to the full board of governors. Wendell Kay represented Mackay before the board. The board decided Mackay should not be disciplined. The case was closed.

In 1964, Neil Mackay was probably one of the wealthiest lawyers in Anchorage; he had a reputation for being obsessed with money, was hard working, sharp, and according to some, at times unethical. Like Nesbett, he'd successfully kicked an alcohol problem acquired in the 1950s. On the ascendency of his real estate career, Mackay would, in the 1970s and 1980s, become embroiled in controversy.

After reading the board of governors' decision in the Mackay case, Nesbett decided to ignore the statutory role of the bar as final arbiter absent an appeal by the lawyer and reopen the case for review by the Supreme Court.

According to Mackay's friend and lawyer, Edgar Paul Boyko, the Supreme Court's targeting of Mackay was ruthless and brutal and started "Mackay on a spiral down" from which he never recovered.

On September 24, Mackay, represented by Wendell Kay and Dave Talbot, appeared before the Supreme Court for a hearing on the old disciplinary case. To many lawyers, the reopening of the case was just one more example of the Supreme Court's overreaching.

On the eve of the federal district court hearing on the bar's case against the Supreme Court, the Supreme Court disbarred Neil Mackay and published its per curiam opinion in the Harland Davis case.

Neither the *Davis* nor *Mackay* decision would help the court's cause.

Too Much to Lose

Going into the federal court hearing, the Supreme Court's position appeared strong. Most state bars around the country were integrated under judicial authority, and the power of courts to integrate bars was well established. But the federal court signaled that it considered Alaska to be a special case since the bar had been created legislatively. Under these circumstances, the federal court was inclined to find that the Alaska Supreme Court could not exercise control over the bar. But both the federal court and the American Bar Association saw that such a decision could set a dangerous precedent, encouraging bar associations across the country to contest judicial control. Because of this, the court and bar received strong encouragement to settle their difference outside of court.

The American Bar Association sent a mediation team to Juneau to work with the Supreme Court and board of governors as the parties met for a settlement conference.

Meanwhile, confident of their position with the federal court, Anchorage bar members petitioned the Alaska Supreme Court to reconsider the *Mackay* case decision.

The Supreme Court granted the petition for rehearing in November and in December came to an agreement with the board of governors on the court-bar fight case. The settlement included state legislation and new bar grievance and admission rules.

A little over a month later, members of the bar ratified the settlement plan, and Ziegler and Nesbett presented a joint statement to the legislature recommending adoption of the new rules. These rules mirrored those in the state of Washington where the bar association conducted the investigation and initial review, providing formal recommendations. There were opportunities to object and respond to the Alaska Supreme Court. On January 29, the Supreme Court rescinded the controversial bar rules and returned funds and files to the Alaska bar. This time the bar accepted its property.

While pieces of the settlement fell into place, Dave Talbot, one of Alaska's co-counsel for the Alaska Bar Association, gushed in a letter to one of the federal district judges that "the miracle I thought couldn't happen is now coming to pass." Talbot added that there "are many members of the Alaska Bar Association who, like myself, are determined that our supreme court will have no occasion to regret this settlement, or to fault the Association for the manner in which it will henceforth discharge the important responsibility of professional self-government."

Talbot's good cheer was somewhat premature. On January 30, as lawyer-legislators John Rader in the House and Howard Pollack in the Senate prepared to introduce settlement legislation, the Supreme Court came down with its final decision in the *Mackay* case and blew the settlement apart.

"Rump" Convention Takes on the Court

Alaska Supreme Court Justice Harry O. Arend wrote the opinion disbarring Neil Mackay. The Anchorage bar was in an uproar. Many lawyers assumed that with the negotiation of new rules for disciplinary action the Supreme Court would dismiss the Mackay case. Mackay had already been exonerated by the bar association. This new Supreme Court decision did not follow the new rules that the court had just agreed to (although the settlement had not yet been implemented by the state legislature). Once again the Supreme Court was unilaterally disciplining a lawyer. The Anchorage bar called for a meeting of the state bar in Anchorage on shortened notice to reconsider the settlement.

In an open letter to lawyers, bar president Ziegler cautioned restraint. He had no intention of hurling a "gauntlet in anyone's face," but urged the bar not to take any action that would derail the settlement.

Ziegler and many other members of the board of governors did not attend the February meeting in Anchorage. Joe Ball, outside counsel, listened quietly as Alaska co-counsel George Boney, David Talbot, and Wendell Kay persuaded colleagues to refuse the settlement. Boney, an avid plaintiffs' lawyer and later Supreme Court justice, took turns with Kay and Talbot (both of whom had represented Neil Mackay) explaining how the *Mackay* decision meant there was no settlement. Lawyers at the meeting voted to reject the settlement and sent this resolution to the board of governors for ratification.

The board of governors met in Juneau to consider the resolutions. Dave Talbot and Wendell Kay, who represented both Mackay and the board in its litigation with the Supreme Court, withdrew as bar counsel. The board, convinced that Kay, Talbot, and Boney had steamrolled the "rump" convention in Anchorage, set aside the resolution. They decided to poll bar members on whether they favored settlement. Ballots came back and, to the surprise of the board members, voted against the settlement.

While lawyers went back to court, the legislature implemented the settlement proposal.

Some lawyers, including Ziegler, pulled out of the case against the court. It was obvious to these lawyers that the fight had now come down to a quest for revenge in the *Mackay* case.

"A Judge Is Supposed to Take It"

Justice Harry O. Arend took Walter Hodge's seat on the Supreme Court when Hodge resigned and was later appointed to the federal district court in 1960. A modest, quiet man, Arend became a member of the Alaska bar in 1934. He had continued to teach high school for a couple of years in Nenana before committing to practice law. In 1936 he moved to nearby Fairbanks and opened a law office.

In March 1965, Justice Arend—who had written the opinion in the *Mackay* case—came up for a public retention vote. Lawyers across the state launched a campaign to vote him off the bench. In Fairbanks, where Arend had practiced for years, television spots opposed the judge. In Juneau, attorneys took to the radio to urge citizens to vote against Arend. In Anchorage, letters sent to clients went like this: "Dear John, I've been your lawyer for a number of years and you've trusted me with your legal problems. Let me tell you what this bench-bar fight means to you." The letter would discuss the bond for jury trials, a threat to the right to a jury trial. It would complain of an imperious Supreme Court's takeover of an independent bar. Finally, it would appeal to the client, as a citizen living in this new state of Alaska, to vote in the forthcoming election for justice and an end to Justice Arend's tenure.

Although deeply hurt by claims that he was obstructing access to jury trials, Arend refused to respond. "A judge is supposed to be a stoic and take it," Arend told Nesbett. He also refused the chief justice's offer to go on the air and explain the situation to the public. After all, it was Nesbett they were really after.

In March 1965, Harry Arend became the first and only Supreme Court justice in the Alaska system to lose office in a vote. The bar, showing its full strength, won its last triumph in the controversy. Later that year, the federal court dismissed without prejudice and without costs the case against the Alaska Supreme Court.

Jay Rabinowitz won appointment to the Alaska Supreme Court, filling Justice Arend's seat. In the years that followed, many who had been prominent in the court-bar fight or had supported it in spirit eventually found their way onto the Supreme Court bench. In 1968, Governor Walter Hickel, taking the advice of his attorney general, Edgar Paul Boyko, forced Nesbett to ask for an expansion of the court to five justices using threats of a budget constraint. The maneuver, according to Boyko, allowed Alaska's first Republican governor to appoint two justices.

Nesbett remembered no threats. But relations between Nesbett and Boyko had been strained ever since Nesbett publicly reprimanded Boyko in a Supreme Court opinion. Nesbett's power base completely eroded with the appointment of George Boney, the dogged bar counsel, and Roger Connor, a liberal lawyer from Juneau. Boney diluted Nesbett's

Five-member Alaska Supreme Court. *Left to right:* Justices John Dimond, Roger Connor, Buell Nesbett, George Boney, and Jay Rabinowitz. Joint archives of the Alaska Court System and the Alaska Bar Association.

power further and enhanced his own by implementing the rotation of the chief justice position among the justices. This meant Nesbett would no longer be the only justice to sit on the Judicial Council and participate in appointments to the bench.

The federal court refused to follow the example of the state court and continued to allow Neil Mackay to practice before its bench. Mackay had a federal practice for a number of years until the state Supreme Court came out with a revised version of the *Mackay* case calling the first decision a mistake and reversing it. John Dimond, the only member of the Supreme Court besides Nesbett who had voted for the original disbarment, wrote the opinion for reinstatement. Fellow justices Boney, Connor, and Rabinowitz, joined the decision, which was published while Nesbett was out of commission and recovering from extensive injuries suffered in a plane crash.

"Dimond thought he saw a chance to become chief justice," Nesbett said of the decision. "It was an illegal decision," he added, since Boney, Connor, and Rabinowitz hadn't been a part of the court at the time of the original case. "Dimond didn't get to be chief justice after all," Nesbett added. "Boney got it."

Although fully reinstated, the experience of being targeted by the Alaska Supreme Court and publicly charged with being "unfit" to be a lawyer and practice before the court left Neil Mackay feeling victimized. Attorney Boyko observed that Mackay "was never quite right" afterward. An eccentric of sorts, Mackay lived with his wife on the top floor of a fourteen-floor building that came to be known as the Mackay Building. A head injury from World War II caused him recurring pain, which he eased with drugs. Divorcing his wife in the mid-1960s, he married a second time and had a son. Both Mackay and his second wife had strong personalities, and the marriage didn't last. A bitter divorce and custody fight finally settled. Afterward, his ex-wife died in a car bombing, and later her brother and executor of her estate was killed in a shooting. The police tried unsuccessfully to tie both deaths to Mackay, who was acquitted of murder charges relating to the death of his former brother-in-law.

Whatever drove Nesbett to reopen the Mackay case and whatever its impact on Mackay professionally and personally, it's impossible to know with any certainty. What is certain is that the loner spirit in Nesbett, which alienated him from the bar, also made it more difficult for him to deal with a Supreme Court no longer within his control. Being a Supreme Court justice changes a person, Nesbett said. "It makes you firm. And you got to be. You won't be the jolly, happy-go-lucky practicing lawyer you were." Taking Alaska out of the territorial era and into a state court system took its toll on Nesbett. He retired from the Supreme Court in 1971.

The Promised Land of Statehood

In the years prior to statehood, most lawyers worked in isolated general practices, looking forward to daily luncheons and frequent socializing, both in court and out, to share their trials and experiences. Although expertise varied among practitioners, a camaraderie pervaded. Most came to Alaska, just as Nesbett did, to escape the constraints and conventions of law practice outside. During the 1950s, bar members supported one another when attacked, as in the *Stringer* case. They served in the territorial legislature, spearheaded the drive to pass the Integrated Bar Act, and worked on the Constitutional Convention, actively participating in, among other things, the drafting of the judiciary article. Although legal practices and agendas varied, attorneys in the 1950s took a leading role in not only shaping the framework for their profession but also the framework for the prospective state of Alaska.

By the end of the 1950s and early 1960s, the bar was becoming less cohesive. More and more lawyers, particularly in Anchorage, formed partnerships, spending long hours behind their desks focused on work for their clients. They had less time for bar lunches, politics, and social activities. The first state court system added another wrinkle, as members of the small coterie of lawyers became elevated to the bench.

In this atmosphere of change and stratification, Buell Nesbett presided over the first Supreme Court and state court system. Few lawyers challenged Nesbett's administrative accomplishments and success in getting the system up and running quickly. Nor did they disagree with Nesbett's goal to improve the legal system and provide reliability and consistency. When the court's idea of improvement came at their expense, though, they protested. When Nesbett took the authority to discipline attorneys, lawyers felt their independence challenged.

Buell Nesbett's tenure as first chief justice demonstrated the difficulties a person at the cusp of two eras, with a foot in each, may encounter moving forward. Nesbett knew well the territorial bar and its factions that operated on the margins, preferring backroom politics and loosely fashioned deals. He'd practiced both politics and law with these customs. He knew how they fought, and at times this knowledge influenced his ability to work productively.

Natural allies became alienated by Nesbett's abrupt efforts to have the bar placed under the control of the judiciary, the taking of bar funds, the arbitrary reopening of the *Mackay* case, and the taking of Harland Davis' petition. That supreme courts in other states had been integrating bar associations for years became lost in a conflict over personalities and power plays.

The court-bar fight was the last time the bar association in Alaska united. The leaders, older members, shared with their younger colleagues the romance of the territorial days. They could whip a group of disparate lawyers into a fighting force with the right cause because those lawyers had come expecting to be on an outpost. In the end, the conflict was an expression both of Alaska's transition into statehood and of the growing professional identity of Alaska's lawyers.

16 ★
Grace
BERG
Schaible
AND THE
Tanana
Valley
BAR

Grace Berg Schaible, a compact woman with short, reddish hair, round face, and ruddy complexion, sat behind her desk in 1982 looking like a partner in a big-city law practice anywhere in the country. Dressed in a tailored suit and matching pumps, Schaible led the Fairbanks-based law firm of Schaible, Staley, DeLisio, and Cook. Direct, analytical, and pragmatic about Fairbanks and Alaska, Schaible reminisced about the people from territorial years with little nostalgia. Though she had her favorites.

Schaible grew up in Juneau, and, at the time of being interviewed, had spent most of her fifty-six years in Alaska. She exhibited a forward-looking confidence rooted in her understanding of Alaska's past and the people who shaped it. She was one of them. Schaible was the first person to be admitted to practice in Alaska's state court in 1959, the first woman to head a traditional, multipartner law firm in Alaska, and the first woman hired as general counsel for a Native corporation. Since the 1982 interview, Schaible continued to collect "firsts": appointed the state's first woman attorney general in 1986, and, some eight years later, the first woman to chair the Alaska Permanent Fund, a multi-billion-dollar investment of Alaska state oil revenue.

Schaible did not dwell on her series of "firsts." She did not consider her gender to be significant to her accomplishments or her career.

Grace Berg Schaible. Anchorage Bar Association Oral History of Territorial Lawyers. Joint Archives of the Alaska Court System and the Alaska Bar Association.

When Alaska lawyers mobilized to remove Justice Harry Arend from the Supreme Court, Grace Berg Schaible balked. She disagreed with Chief Justice Buell Nesbett's high-handed tactics, but unlike her colleagues, she firmly refused to let Justice Arend take the fall. She felt that "Harry Arend should strike out on his own and tell Buell Nesbett to go to hell." Of course, she acknowledged, it would have been impossible for an associate justice to publicly call out the chief justice. That just left Arend as much a victim of Nesbett as the bar.

Schaible refused to pay the extra dues the bar members collected to wage war against this surrogate for Chief Justice Nesbett. Instead, she quietly supported the movement that stood up for her fellow Fairbanksian. You were "considered an absolute idiot, a boob, a stupid, incompetent human being for being in favor of Harry Arend," Schaible said.

It wouldn't be the first time that Schaible parted company with established thinking.

Grace Berg was born on November 28, 1925, into a Juneau immigrant family. Her father came to the United States from Norway and traveled to Alaska in 1912 to look for gold in the Chistochina country north of Cordova. He didn't find gold but did fall in love with Juneau and southeast Alaska that so reminded him of the land he'd left. Five years later he married a woman who had emigrated from Sweden, and together they began to raise their family in Juneau.

In the small Juneau society, Grace Berg grew up with the under-standing that those most respected, people of integrity and character, included personnel from the Juneau gold mine, doctors, bankers, and, of course, lawyers.

Schaible remembered how her parents characterized different law-yers, and later observed how she carried these early prejudices as a child. Grover Winn was not considered a very good lawyer because he drank too much. Michael Monagle had a reputation for being a sharp lawyer, a comment not meant in the nicest way, and in the early years his Roman Catholicism did not endear him to northern European immigrants. But the most prejudicial slur that she remembered hearing involved the sole Native attorney in Juneau, William Paul, who had a practice with William Steele. Schaible remembered her father's rejoinder when Paul's name came up: Will Paul Will Steele (as in steal).

Schaible formed her own opinion of Paul many years later. She remembered Paul being one of the first to congratulate her when she began practicing law in the late 1950s. According to Schaible, Paul com-mented on how nice it was to see a woman practicing.

"For the last twenty-five years, thirty years, I've really admired Will Paul," Schaible said in 1997. "To me he was a very warm human being, someone who's tenacity I admired." Schaible credited Paul, along with his son Frederick Paul, with organizing Native support and laying the foundation for the landmark Alaska Native Claims Settlement Act. The act, which established Alaska Native corporate ownership and control of most tribal lands in the state, would have taken much longer to pass without Paul's help, according to Schaible.

William Paul was not the only lawyer practicing in Juneau during the 1930s and 1940s who was not accepted within the established order. Schaible remembered Mildred Hermann garnering little respect from her Republican peers because she'd gotten her law degree from a LaSalle correspondence school. "They either liked them to clerk for an attorney they respected or a judge," Schaible observed.

Hermann, who had to take the bar three times before examiners finally passed her, entered the practice in 1934. "Mildred was a real pio-neer," Schaible said. "I admired her grit and determination."

Graduating from Juneau High School in 1943, Schaible took two years off before going to college. During this time, she met Dr. Charles Bunnell, president of Alaska's Agricultural College and School of Mines in Fairbanks (now known as the University of Alaska). Dr. Bunnell—

who would become a mentor and friend—convinced Schaible to travel to Fairbanks to do her undergraduate work rather than to Northwestern University in Chicago, where she'd been accepted.

Charles Bunnell and Fairbanks

Schaible saw Fairbanks for the first time in September 1945, when she arrived to start school. From the air, Fairbanks looked spectacular, with gold leaves on dark trees. But when she stepped off the plane the streets were filled with mud. While the town itself was very small, with fewer than 5,000 people, Eielson Air Force Base, under construction outside of town to accommodate World War II, was quite large. Construction had just begun on Ladd Field, and the war was winding down. Russians still traveled through Fairbanks piloting US airplanes under the lend-lease program, but not as frequently as during the height of the war.

The difference between Juneau's mild maritime climate and Fairbanks' harsh interior climate went a long way toward defining the difference among those who chose to make one or the other home.

Schaible found Fairbanksians, like their weather, to be tough and hardy. They didn't grouse about the dark and cold of winter where temperatures hovered at 50 below and the sun barely made an appearance. And they thoroughly enjoyed the summers where temperatures climbed into the 70s and 80s and the sun stayed out past midnight.

"It was a mining community," Schaible said. "But it was a different mining community than I grew up in." Juneau's hard rock mining took place underground and employed many immigrant laborers. In Fairbanks, placer mining kept miners—many of them mining engineers—above ground, dredging for gold.

Although Fairbanks, too, had the pronounced social stratification common to small towns—with doctors, lawyers, merchants, and prosperous miners on top—Eielson Air Force Base, with its constant turnover in military personnel, lent a transience to the population. The University of Alaska also influenced Fairbanks' character. Schaible noted that at one time Fairbanks had the greatest number of college graduates per capita in the country.

During her four years at the university, Schaible served as Bunnell's secretary, and the two developed a father-daughter relationship.

When Schaible worked for Bunnell in the 1940s, he was well into his sixties and nearing retirement. He'd grown up in Pennsylvania and traveled to Alaska in 1900, where he worked as a teacher and lawyer.

In 1915, he was appointed federal district court judge in Fairbanks. Six years later, in 1921, he left the bench and became president of the university.

Bunnell told Schaible stories from his many years in the territory. Sometimes, as he got older and developed diabetes, he'd forget that she was not his contemporary and talk to her of people long dead. Schaible stayed a year after graduation to help with the transition as Bunnell became president emeritus of the university and a new president took his place. Then, after a year of building up her finances, she took off for Washington, DC, and George Washington University's graduate school of government.

She continued to stay in contact with Bunnell, and a voluminous correspondence developed between the two. He visited her in Washington, DC, and she him in Fairbanks. "He was a very lonely man," Schaible said, and "a person I was so close to at a very important time in my life." Although objective about many she's dealt with, Schaible admits that it is hard for her to be objective about Bunnell, with whom she developed such a close friendship.

The correspondence between the two often turned to the statehood movement and the direction of Alaska. Schaible remembered the early 1950s as an extremely exciting time to be in Washington, DC, especially since she knew—from growing up in Juneau and living in Alaska—many of the Alaskans working with Congress to further the statehood movement. She had breakfast with Alaska Governor Frank Heintzleman when he was in town and often went to Alaska Delegate Bob Bartlett and his wife's home for dinner. Between these meetings and her correspondence with Bunnell, Schaible closely followed the politics of the 1950s.

Schaible returned to Alaska during the summer months to work on her master's thesis, which dealt with the territorial legislature. In 1953, she took a job in Juneau with the newly established legislative council aiding legislators in writing territorial law. She met territorial lawyers, including Wendell Kay, Tom Stewart, Paul Robison, and Robert McNealy, who came down to Juneau for the sixty-day sessions. Schaible found it difficult to write legislation without having been to law school. Lawyers in the legislature, respectful of her determination, suggested she go to law school. She applied and was accepted at Yale Law School.

When she graduated from law school, Schaible knew she wanted to go into private practice with a firm, but it wouldn't be in Juneau. "The law firms in Juneau hardly ever hired the locals," Schaible observed, the exception being Roger Connor. Schaible also did not want to hang out her own shingle.

By the late 1950s it wasn't nearly as difficult for women to enter the legal practice as it had been for Mildred Hermann in 1934. Schaible ticked off the names of women lawyers she remembered practicing at the time, including Dorothy Awes Haaland, Dorothy Tyner, Mary Alice Miller, and M. Ashley Dickerson. Tyner and Miller would become the first two female judges in Alaska. Appointed in 1968, Tyner became a district court judge in Anchorage and Miller, district court judge in Fairbanks.

Women Practicing Law in Alaska in the 1950s

Before I started to study law, a woman told me I had a wonderful opportunity.
She was right, it was much more rewarding than playing bridge.
—Gladys Stabler Wynd (member of Alaska bar, 1951)

Gladys Stabler (later Wynd) graduated from the University of Oregon with a Master of Arts in Mathematics in 1928. She studied law in the office of her husband, Juneau attorney Howard Stabler, from 1943 to 1951, when she was admitted to the bar. The two practiced together as partners until his death in 1963. Gladys continued as a partner in Stabler, Gregg & Meuwissen (later Kohls) in Juneau until her retirement in 1968. She had mostly an office practice, including probate work. Joint archives of the Alaska Court System and the Alaska Bar Association.

Juliana "Jan" Wilson (*back row, far left*) graduated from the University of North Carolina law school in 1950 at the same time as her husband T. Stanton Wilson. She worked for J. L. McCarrey Jr. before he was appointed to the bench. McCarrey mentored Wilson and encouraged her to practice law. Upon McCarrey's appointment to the bench, Wilson bought his practice. She and her husband established the Wilson and Wilson law firm in Anchorage. They practiced until 1980, when they went into semiretirement. Their practice was mostly civil, including real estate, probate, and corporate. *Back row, left to right:* Juliana D. Wilson, Hannah Wetmore, J. L. McCarrey Jr., Cora McCarrey, Florence Sessoms, unknown. *Front row, left to right:* unknown, Rachel Patterson, Margaret Kish, unknown. Joint archives of the Alaska Court System and the Alaska Bar Association.

Women lawyers at the International Women's Day luncheon, March 8, 1999. *Sitting, left to right:* M. Ashley Dickerson and Juliana "Jan" Wilson. *Standing, left to right:* Susan Reeves, Grace Schaible, Esther Wunnicke. Courtesy Barbara Hood, Joint archives of the Alaska court System and the Alaska Bar Association.

M. Ashley Dickerson: Tough Adversary

Like her classmate and lifelong friend Rosa Parks, M. Ashley Dickerson never let the way things were stand in the way of working to make them better.

Born in 1912 in Montgomery, Alabama, Dickerson was the first African American woman admitted to practice law in Alaska. Before practicing law in Alaska, she was the first African American woman admitted to the Alabama bar and second African American admitted to practice in Indiana.

A graduate of Fisk University in 1935 and Howard University School of Law in 1948, Dickerson studied with the late US Supreme Court Justice Thurgood Marshall.

In 1959, divorced and with three teenage sons, Dickerson traveled to Alaska and opened a law office in Anchorage's Fairview neighborhood. Her passion for justice, strong will, and determination made her a public figure for much of her nearly fifty-year career in the state. Known to most as "M. Ashley," she focused on civil cases, especially those dealing with civil rights and discrimination.

"I had very few black clients at first," Dickerson said in a 1998 interview, "because black people thought there was something magic about a white attorney. I started getting black clients only after I started winning cases against some of their white attorneys."

Flamboyant and outspoken, Dickerson understood that being an outsider in the legal community had its advantages. "Sometimes folks would call and say, 'I know I can trust you because I know you won't be having cocktails with the other attorney tonight or coffee in the morning.'"

One much-told story involved Dickerson's appearance in court in a pantsuit, before women were permitted to wear them in court. The judge admonished her and told her to come back in more suitable attire. She returned in a ball gown, with a feathered hat on her head.

"Ms. Dickerson developed a reputation for being independent and fearless—a tough adversary for anyone who stood in the way of what she thought was right. Few who encountered her made the mistake of dismissing her because of her gender or her race," said Alaska Supreme Court Justice Dana Fabe.

In 1983, Dickerson became the first African American president of the National Association of Women Lawyers. She would later receive one of the American Bar Association's most prestigious awards, the Margaret Brent Award. The award recognized women lawyers who had achieved professional excellence in their fields and paved the way to success for other women lawyers.

Schaible Develops Fairbanks Practice

Schaible, at first, planned to go to Anchorage and practice with lawyers she'd worked with in the territorial legislature. She changed her plans when she got a better offer from Dr. Arthur Schaible in Fairbanks.

Dr. Schaible, quite a bit older than Grace, had long practiced medicine in Fairbanks and among Alaska Natives in rural Alaska. The two married on Christmas Day in 1958.

Schaible credited Fairbanks with providing opportunities she could not have had elsewhere in Alaska. "I probably never would have become a partner in a law firm in Anchorage," she said. Fairbanks also provided a greater range of legal work and access to clients than Schaible believed she could have had in Anchorage.

Schaible represented the University of Alaska and served as general counsel for the Arctic Slope Regional Corporation during these years. She is certain that these opportunities would not have been available to her had she started out in Anchorage. The prejudices of Anchorage's older, established firms, and of Alaska Natives, she believed, would have interfered.

But Fairbanks was different.

In Fairbanks, Schaible's partners had developed good relationships with Alaska Natives. Her husband, too, was well known among Alaska Native communities. "He grew up without any prejudices," Schaible said. Fairbanks made it easier for people to get to know you and trust you. Anchorage's size made that more difficult, according to Schaible.

Schaible, among the first group of lawyers admitted to practice after Alaska became a state, joined the Fairbanks firm of McNealy, Merdes, Camarot and Fitzgerald in 1959. Although the firm was situated in Fairbanks, all of the lawyers had worked in Juneau at one time or another in their careers, including in the attorney general's office, US attorney's office, legislature, and governor's office.

McNealy, the lead partner, had been practicing in Alaska the longest, since 1947, and had been Senate president. He specialized in probate work and was a patient teacher, Schaible said, though a drinking problem sometimes interfered with his work.

"I was always very disappointed that he just couldn't stay off the booze," Schaible said. His partners periodically escorted him to a recovery program in Washington State frequented by other Alaskans.

Heavy drinking plagued a number of members of the Fairbanks Tanana Valley Bar. Schaible remembered attending parties and picnics organized by the bar and having to get the more inebriated members into cars and have others drive them home. She recalled that Warren William Taylor, later Fairbanks Superior Court judge, used to be "absolutely super," making sure the incapacitated members didn't get picked up by state troopers.

Schaible became a named partner in her Fairbanks firm seven years after starting. In 1983, the firm became Schaible, Staley, DeLisio, and Cook—the first traditional, multipartner law firm in Alaska to have a woman lead partner.

Looking back, Bunnell's advice had proven right. It would be Fairbanks where Schaible could go as far as her ambition, talent, and skill would take her. It would be Fairbanks, where people took pride in living in a place of extremes and knowing their neighbors well, a place that valued individuality, where one of Alaska's most successful attorneys would call home.

17 ★
MORE
Frontier
STORIES

One of the most frequently told stories among territorial lawyers is that of Fred Crane and the Nome bar convention.

Crane, a longtime lawyer from the interior, had been disbarred for drinking up a number of his clients' estates. In the 1950s, with the aid of Fairbanks attorney Warren Taylor, Crane was reinstated on the condition that he confine his practice to Nome—although in no time at all, Crane was helping out in Taylor's Fairbanks office.

In the late 1960s, Crane invited the Alaska Bar Association to hold its annual convention in Nome. He promised to put on a show that members would never forget. Unfortunately, he wasn't there to see it. A couple of months before the convention, Fred Crane died.

With all the arrangements in place, with even a federal court judge scheduled to speak, the convention went on as planned. Lawyers traveled to Nome, and when it came time to pick the federal judge up at the airport, a group drove out to meet him. Unfortunately, no one knew what the judge looked like. They picked up the one man who came off the airplane wearing a suit. They wined and dined their guest. When he got up to speak to the group at the Sunday banquet, he thanked everyone for their warm welcome and launched into a discussion of the merits of dried milk, which he'd come to Nome to peddle. He had never expected such an enthusiastic reception.

The highlight of the convention, however, came on the Saturday night before the banquet. Lawyers got together for the traditional all-night poker game and drinking. Waxing nostalgic over the premature death of Fred Crane, someone mentioned that no one could be buried in Nome during the winter months. All the bodies were kept in storage until the ground thawed. Should they go get Fred and prop him up at their table for one last toast? Some remember Fred Crane joining them that evening, while others are certain that it was just Crane's spirit that entered the smoky room.

This popular story started nearly a decade after statehood. Territorial lawyers and those who'd come to the new state relish the telling, a story proving still the unique qualities of Alaska and the community of lawyers among whom they practiced.

Lawyers who came to Alaska before statehood sought not a place rushing to catch up with the conventions they'd left, but a place offering something different. Alaska did not disappoint.

Wendell Kay could leave behind his father's staid Midwestern practice and pattern himself after the great gold rush trial attorney George Grigsby. Weatherman Norman Banfield could escape the grip of the Depression and use his capacity for hard work and attention to detail to gain financial security and prestige as a lawyer with partner H. L. Faulkner. Buell Nesbett could turn down a big San Francisco law firm to practice with Anchorage's John Manders, who refused to pay his income tax, and Stanley McCutcheon, who never attended law school—and go on to become the first chief justice of the Alaska Supreme Court.

The majority of Alaska's territorial lawyers were white and male, just as their counterparts outside of Alaska. Those who were not faced barriers to practice. Were there more opportunities for women lawyers in Alaska than outside of Alaska? Were the women who were attracted to Alaska more independent minded and more likely to find opportunity in the territory and state? The sample is small, making it too difficult to generalize. What we can say is that women like Mildred Hermann, Dorothy Awes Haaland, Grace Berg Schaible, and M. Ashley Dickerson contributed much to Alaska, probably more than their number would suggest.

William Paul, the first Alaska Native lawyer, leaves a legacy of accomplishment and advocacy, as well as controversy. The shadow of racism so endemic in Alaska falls heavily upon his legal career.

Still, Alaska's territorial lawyers, whether they were white, male, female, Alaska Native, or African American, experienced the novelty and unpredictability of practicing in a place different from the rest

Nesbett Courthouse in Anchorage. Courtesy of Pamela Cravez.

of the United States. Each, in their way, fulfilled the needs of small Alaskan communities by practicing law and often doing much more. They served on school boards and in the territorial legislature. They founded banks, fought for statehood, lobbied for equal rights, and worked on writing the constitution for a new state. Not all lawyers participated on a broader scale. Not all supported the same causes. Often lawyers carried the same prejudices and narrow-mindedness of their communities. They also carried the most forward-looking ideas.

Alaska's territorial lawyers shared the conviction that their individuality and independence meant more than their profession. During the 1950s harbingers of change—more people, more lawyers, and statehood—threatened the easygoing territorial practice. Lawyers traded in some of their individuality and independence for greater control over their profession. The Integrated Bar Act of 1955 formalized a hierarchy among lawyers with the creation of the Alaska Bar Association's board of governors. The Constitutional Convention set up a judicial selection system based upon merit that gave lawyers an important role in determining the makeup of the state judiciary. These efforts provided lawyers some control as Alaska barreled toward statehood and a new state court system.

The Missouri Plan adopted at Alaska's Constitutional Convention in 1955 paved the way for a merit system of appointing judges in Alaska. At the time it was adopted, there were few lawyers in Alaska. The first go at selecting judges reflected the small pool of lawyers who knew one another well.

Now there are roughly 4,000 members of the Alaska bar. The Missouri system for selecting judges and providing information to the public at the time of judicial retention elections has become refined and systemic. According to Justice Rabinowitz, it's made the bench "accessible to those who aren't from old-time families, who aren't politically connected, who aren't wealthy, and have no power base. . . . It's made it accessible to talented lawyers."

In 1964, lawyers young and old signed their names to the Alaska Bar Association's suit against the Alaska Supreme Court. In a last hurrah, they signaled their ability to still be roused as a group to challenge authority and to be independent. For good or ill, they convinced their clients, neighbors, and friends that Justice Harry Arend should be voted out of office for his part in the court-bar fight.

Like the story of Fred Crane, the court-bar fight is a vestige from the Alaska bar's territorial identity, an identity long gone. More than one hundred years after the gold rushes, nearly sixty years after statehood, the face of Alaska and its lawyers looks much like its lower forty-eight counterparts. Names like Nesbett and Boney grace state courthouses in Anchorage. Few remember the personalities from territorial years, their firms dissolved, and more flamboyant trial lawyers are making headlines. Each year another group of lawyers enters the bar, creating more and more distance from that past community where lawyers knew each other so well, sometimes too well.

Still, stop lawyers on the street and ask if they think they're living on the frontier. Odds are they will say, "Yes." Perhaps it's the distance between Alaska and the rest of the United States, the comparatively small population, or the rugged Chugach Mountains outside law office windows. They'll say that they feel a greater sense of independence, individuality, and ability to define their own practice in Alaska than where they've left. And, they will tell you their own "frontier" stories.

Afterword

I began this work more than thirty years ago, when I came to Alaska with my boyfriend (now husband) the summer of 1980. We'd both been going to law school on the East Coast—I was studying in Washington, DC, at Catholic University and Glenn in North Carolina at Duke. Glenn always wanted to see Alaska and had a summer internship with the Anchorage law firm Ely, Guess, and Rudd. I thought Alaska would be a great summer adventure.

I went to the courthouse my second day in town and checked the job board in the law library. A person steered me to the district attorney's office. By the end of the day, I'd spoken with Larry Weeks, the Anchorage district attorney, and had a job for the summer.

The differences between what I saw of the legal profession that summer compared to what I'd experienced while living in Washington, DC, were startling. No stuffy law firms with hundreds of lawyers dressed in dark suits working around the clock. Lawyers in Alaska were more interested in talking about their adventures outside the office than the nuances of cases or arguments. In the district attorneys' office a couple of lawyers had private pilot's licenses. One had returned from a year's trip around the world. Another flew on small bush planes to the Aleutian Islands to prosecute cases. She confided that she had been chosen for this duty since she was the only assistant district attorney at the time without a husband or children.

Russ Arnett in 1982. Anchorage Bar Association Oral History of Territorial Lawyers, Pamela Cravez. Joint archives of the Alaska Court System and the Alaska Bar Association.

I look back at this summer experience as my initiation into how things are done differently in Alaska. Until then I'd only seen my fellow law students competing for jobs with big prestigious law firms, vying for clerkships with judges on the East Coast, or looking for government jobs. Many of the lawyers I met that summer were just as competitive, just as sharp, but seemed to have found a place where they had an opportunity to create more balance between their professional and private lives. Not something people were talking much about in the 1980s.

I asked the district attorney who could tell me more about the practice of law in Alaska? He suggested I speak with Russ Arnett, the unofficial Alaska bar historian.

Arnett had an unhurried way about him and calm blue eyes. His face, tanned from daily walks, made him look much younger than his mid-fifties. He was reluctant to talk of the practice of law in Alaska. My enthusiasm for the novelty of what I'd been experiencing put him off.

"This isn't the frontier anymore," Arnett said.

A graduate of Northwestern Law School, Arnett arrived in Alaska in 1952 to become commissioner in Nome when his friend, James von der Heydt, vacated the position.

"Lawyers just want to work for big firms, no different from anywhere else," Arnett said nearly 40 years later. Although lawyers think that they are escaping the grinding routine of big city practice, they bring that routine with them, he added.

He picked up a stack of Xeroxed pages stapled together and handed them to me. Each sheet had a copy of a story he'd written about territorial lawyers for the *Alaska Bar Rag*, the Alaska Bar Association's newspaper.

The floating court, the first state court system, flying and fishing trips among lawyers, and the court-bar fight were among Arnett's work. Each article provided a quick sketch of colorful exploits and hyperbolic characters. The essays spared names and avoided speaking ill of fellow practitioners. Arnett's generosity in sharing stories started me on this work. His articles hinted at the unique qualities of Alaska's territorial practice and how quickly they'd disappeared.

Federal District Court Judge James Fitzgerald's passion for Alaska history, especially its legal history, is well known. He was an early champion of the oral history project. So was attorney Bob Ely, who came to Alaska in 1959.

As a new lawyer and new to Alaska, I depended upon a number of people to help me better understand the personalities and politics of Alaska's territorial and early state bar. Among those providing insight were Roger Cremo, John Rader, Superior Court Judge Victor Carlson, and Superior Court Judge Tom Stewart.

Stewart, born in Juneau, secretary to the Constitutional Convention, and first administrator for the Alaska Supreme Court, devoted his life to serving Alaska and Alaskans. Probably more than any other person I spoke with, Stewart was determined to create a historical record of Alaska's transition to statehood. He knew the value of collecting all perspectives and the importance of the time during which he'd lived and worked. His contributions to Alaska are immense and worthy of greater telling.

This work stops at the transition to statehood, touching only briefly upon the important role that lawyers have had in developing the legal framework for the state of Alaska. As Justice Rabinowitz noted when interviewed in 2000, "No one teaches you how to become a state and what you need to do to be a state." Rabinowitz came to Alaska in 1957 as a law clerk for territorial judge Vernon Forbes, and went on to become an assistant attorney general and Supreme Court justice.

Superior Court Judge Thomas "Tom" Stewart in 1982. Anchorage Bar Association Oral History of Territorial Lawyers, Pamela Cravez. Joint archives of the Alaska Court System and the Alaska Bar Association.

"Young, very remarkable attorneys" helped set up the offices and systems necessary for Alaska to function as a state. Few lawyers in modern times have had the privilege of living through the transition from territory to state, Rabinowitz said. Lawyers responsible for easing Alaska's passage through its first fifty years include Rabinowitz, Rader, Assistant Attorney General George Hayes, John Havelock, and Bob Erwin, to name but a few.

Dorothy Awes Haaland, one of the first lawyers I interviewed, became a friend. I admired this progressive and passionate advocate and her work in support of women and equal rights. Her husband, Ragnar, was a true partner. They shared a love for learning and ideas and a devotion to human rights.

Although we spoke many times, Dorothy never mentioned feeling that her gender had impacted her ability to practice law. She was proud of what she'd accomplished in Alaska, a place so different from anywhere else in the country.

I know that even though she did not speak of prejudice, it was there.

Since I began this project in the 1980s, more information has become available about Alaska's territorial lawyers. The state court law library archives is filled with files and boxes of materials. Much of this is due to the hard work of the Alaska Bar Association Historians Committee. Alaska law archivist Nancy Tileston has been tireless in her efforts to help me review as much as I could while preparing this manuscript.

I suspect that there is no one more knowledgeable about Alaska legal history than Leroy Barker. His enthusiasm and energy have encouraged many, including myself. I greatly appreciate his review of this manuscript.

Marilyn May, who like Leroy, has chaired the Historians Committee, helped with permission for photos and access to materials with great efficiency that is much appreciated.

Information about Alaska's female attorneys continues to grow. Thanks to Barbara Hood both for her review of this work and the valuable information she has collected on Alaska's women lawyers. Phyllis Demuth Movius' book, *A Place of Belonging: Five Founding Women of Fairbanks, Alaska* featured two lawyers for which there had previously been little written: Nathalena Roberts Moore and Dr. Aline Beegler.

There is much still to be learned about the diversity of lawyers – not just female lawyers – who've practiced in Alaska and their impact on our justice system.

Many thanks to Yvonne Wu Goldsmith and Averil Lerman, who reviewed early drafts. Yvonne, reviewing in record speed and filling in information, also helped me better understand where I needed to explain things more clearly for nonlawyers.

Alaska legal historian Averil Lerman, an expert on capital punishment in territorial Alaska, provided insight on 1940s and 1950s Juneau that was particularly helpful. Her review of this manuscript improved it greatly.

Finally, thanks to my husband, Glenn who has long understood the importance of balance in life.

Notes

Introduction

1. Jay Rabinowitz, oral history conducted by Ron Inouye in 2000, University of Alaska Fairbanks, Jukebox. "In Territorial days, when I first came to Fairbanks, we had . . . Jack Mahler had just beaten the US Attorney's Office in Fairbanks on a tax evasion case. He was defended by Ed Boyko. Do you know that name? All right, Ed Boyko used the Patrick Henry defense of no taxation without representation. We didn't have a vote in those days for the President . . . we were a Territory, right. And the jury loved it—not guilty. And it became known as the Jack Mahler defense."

Chapter 1

1. Charles C. Hawley, Alaska Mining Hall of Fame, Jafet Lindeberg, http://www.alaskamininghalloffame.org/inductees/lindeberg.php, 1998.

2. Kenneth O. Bjork, "Reindeer, Gold, and Scandal," Norwegian-American History Association, NAHA online, vol. 30, p. 130, http://www.naha.stolaf.edu/pubs/nas/volume30/vol30_05.htm.

3. Charles C. Hawley, Alaska Mining Hall of Fame, John Brynteson, http://www.alaskamininghalloffame.org/inductees/brynteson.php, 1998.

4. Charles C. Hawley, Alaska Mining Hall of Fame, Erik Lindblom, http://www.alaskamininghalloffame.org/inductees/lindblom.php, 1998.

5. William R. Morrow, "The Spoilers," 2 *California Law Review* 89 (1916).

6. State Historical Society of North Dakota, Lesson 4: Alliances and Conflicts; Topic 5: Bosses and Reformers; Section 2: Alexander McKenzie, Includes McKenzie obituary, cartoon, and description. http://ndstudies.gov/gr8/content/unit-iii-waves-development-1861-1920/lesson-4-alliances-and-conflicts/topic-5-bosses-and-reformers/section-2-alexander-mckenzie.

7. Dan Plazak, *A Hole in the Ground with a Liar at the Top: Fraud and Deceit in the Golden Age of American Mining* (Salt Lake City: University of Utah Press, 2006).

8. Cornelius William Gillam Hyde, Clement A. Lounsberry, Hugh McGrath, and William Stoddard, *History of the Great Northwest and Its Men of Progress* (Minneapolis: Minneapolis Journal, 1901).

9. Curt Eriksmoen, "Grand Forks Attorney, Others, Involved in Gold Swindle," *Bismarck Tribune*, March 20, 2010.

10. *Tornanses v. Melsing* et al.; *Kjellman v. Rogers*, 1 *Alaska Federal Reports* 639, 106 F. 775 (1901).

11. Id., at pp. 649–50.

12. Id., at p. 655.

13. Id., at p. 662.

14. *In re Alexander McKenzie*, 180 U.S. 536 (1901).

15. James Wickersham, *Old Yukon, Tales-Trails-Trials* (Washington, DC: Washington Law Book, 1938), 365 (Nome lawyers getting along with Noyes and not).

16. Evangeline Atwood, *Frontier Politics: Alaska's James Wickersham* (Portland, OR: Binford and Mort, 1979), 90.

17. Ibid., 83.

18. Rex Beach, "The Looting of Alaska: The True Story of a Robbery by Law," *Appleton's Booklovers Magazine*, vol. 6, January 1906.

Chapter 2

1. Wickersham, *Old Yukon: Tales-Trails-Trials*, 83.

2. William R. Hunt, *Distant Justice: Policing the Alaska Frontier* (Norman: University of Oklahoma Press, 1987), 101.

3. Atwood, *Frontier Politics*, 31, quoting the *Seattle Daily Times*, June 17, 1889.

4. Wickersham, *Old Yukon: Tales-Trails-Trials*, 366.

5. Hunt, *Distant Justice*, 124.

Chapter 3

1. Hunt, *Distant Justice*, 132, detailing Colonel Melvin Grigsby's tenure as US attorney in Nome.

2. Atwood, *Frontier Politics*, 118, quoting Wickersham Diary, February 10, 1904.

3. Hunt, *Distant Justice*, 141–43, Jolley case.

4. *Nome Semi-Weekly News*, June 12, 1903, p. 4.

5. *Valdez Miner*, May 4, 1918; Hunt, *Distant Justice*, 132.

6. Author interview with Robert Ziegler, April 19, 1982, Anchorage Bar Association, Oral History of Alaska's Territorial Lawyers (hereafter OHTL).

7. Author interview with John Hellenthal, May 15, 1982, OHTL.

8. Author interview with Ret. Anchorage Superior Court Judge Harold Butcher, 1983.

9. Author interview with Judge Ralph Moody, November 3, 1982, OHTL.

Chapter 4

1. Author interview of Norman Banfield, April 21, 1982, OHTL. All Banfield quotes and recollections in this chapter are from this interview.

2. Donald Craig Mitchell, *Sold American: A Story of Alaska Natives and Their Land* (Fairbanks: University of Alaska Press, 1997), 255.

3. Chicken Ridge Historic Building Survey, City/Borough of Juneau, September 1992.

4. *Alaska Weekly*, January 23, 1931, pp. 6–8.

5. Letter of R. N. De Armond to author, January 20, 1984.

6. The first division judge routinely held sessions of court in Juneau, Wrangel, and Sitka, although the only courthouse was built in Juneau.

7. David G. Stone, "Herbert Lionel Faulkner," Alaska Mining Hall of Fame, 2007, http://www.alaskamininghalloffame.org/inductees/faulkner.php.

8. Ibid.

9. In 1946, the court was paying up to $200 for an appeal, according to Averil Lerman's research on death penalty cases in territorial Alaska.

10. $33 of the Merchant Marine Act of 1920, now $30104, Title 46 of the United States Code.

11. Stephen W. Haycox, "William Paul, Sr., and the Alaska Voters' Literacy Act of 1925," *Alaska History* 2, no. 1 (Winter 1986/87): 17–38.

12. Terrence M. Cole, "Jim Crow in Alaska: The Passage of the Alaska Equal Rights Act of 1945," in *An Alaska Anthology: Interpreting the Past*, ed. Stephen Haycox and Mary Childers Mangusso (Seattle: University of Washington Press, 1996), 314–35.

13. Mitchell, *Sold American*, 221–86. For a discussion of William Paul and his political influence.

14. Ibid.

15. The Faulkner Banfield firm represented Alaska Natives to a greater extent after statehood.

16. *U.S. ex. Rel. Folta v. Paul*, 9 Alaska 189 (1937).

17. Id., at p. 145.

18. Id., at p. 195.

19. LaRue Hellenthal, "Hellenthal," Juneau-Douglas City Museum. http://juneau.org/parkrec/museum/forms/GCM/readarticle.php?UID=886&newxtkey.

20. Avrum Gross interviewed by author April 2, 1997. "Norman decided that he would figure out who made the money in the firm. It was stunning because what happened, I think, was [Robert] Boochever made the most money, then I made the next most money, then Mike Holmes made the next most money, and then you got way down and there was Norman. I mean he didn't make a lot of money in the firm. Which affected none of us. None of us cared, or even gave it

a moment's thought. Norman wasn't honored for the money he brought in, he was honored for the way he ran the firm, the kind of standards he imposed and for the history he brought with him."

Chapter 5

1. W. C. Arnold interviewed February 11, 1982, and February 27, 1982.

2. Pamela Cravez, *Seizing the Frontier: Alaska's Territorial Lawyers* (1984).

3. Burton Biss interviewed December 30, 1982, Cravez, *Territorial Lawyers*, transcript, pp. 29–31.

4. 37 Stat. 512., Sec. 3.

5. White Act of 1924.

6. Richard Cooley, *Politics and Conservation: The Decline of the Alaska Salmon* (New York: Harper and Row, 1963), 35.

7. Ibid., 145.

8. Ibid., 135–36.

9. Author interview with Banfield, April 21, 1982, OHTL.

Chapter 6

1. Information about Haaland was first published in a profile by the author, *Feminist Freedom Fighter*, that appeared in the *Anchorage Daily News* magazine, *We Alaskans*, March 6, 1982.

2. "Lawyer by Accident," by Mildred R. Hermann, Juneau, Alaska (Alaska's only female lawyer) 27 *Women Law J* 7 (1940–41).

3. Ibid., 7.

4. Kristin Boraas, "Mildred Robinson Hermann: Queen Mother of the Alaskan Statehood," 27 *AK Bar Rag* 32 (May–June 2003). Boraas telephone interview with Judge Thomas Stewart (October 25, 2000) cited.

5. Cravez, *Seizing the Frontier: Alaska's Territorial Lawyers*, 61.

6. 27 *Women's Law J* 7, p. 8.

7. Grace H. Harte, "The One Woman Lawyer of Alaska," 27 *Women's Lawyers Journal* 16 (1940–41): 16

8. Burnita Shelton Matthew, "The Woman Juror," *Women Lawyers Journal* 15, no. 2 (January 1927), wlh.law.stanford.edu/wp-content/uploads/2011/01/the-woman-juror-15wlj151927.pdf. The Civil Rights Act of 1957 gave women the right to sit on federal juries.

9. *Taylor v. Louisiana*, 419 U.S. 522 (1975).

10. Information about Isabel Ambler Gilman was provided to the author from R. N. De Armond in 1984. Information about the first two women lawyers to practice in Fairbanks is from two articles published by Fairbanks historian Phyllis Demuth Movius: "Another Candidate for Alaska's First Woman Lawyer Nathalena Roberts Moore, 1875–1950," *Alaska Bar Rag* (July–September 2004); "Early Woman Attorney Pioneers Reform in Fairbanks, Aline Chenot Baskerville Bradley Beegler, 1867–1943," *Alaska Bar Rag* (January–March 2004).

11. Ibid.

12. Mention of Gilman practicing law in Seldovia is in the *Granite Monthly*, vol. 46 (January–December 1914).

13. Ibid.; Movius, "Another Candidate for Alaska's First Woman Lawyer" and "Early Woman Attorney Pioneers Reform in Fairbanks."

14. Claus-M. Naske, *Alaska: A History of the 49th State*, 2nd ed. (Norman: University of Oklahoma Press, 1987).

15. Ibid.

16. Movius, "Early Woman Attorney Pioneers Reform in Fairbanks."

17. Ibid.; Dr. Dora Fugard, 1903, was the first female doctor in Alaska.

18. Ibid.

19. Ibid.

20. Ibid.

21. There may be other women who have been admitted to the Alaska bar.

22. Ibid.; Haaland interview.

23. "Lawyer by Accident," 9.

24. Ibid., p. 37.

25. City of Cordova, Alaska, Cordova Fast Fact, History, www.cityofcordova. net.

26. Author interview with Russ Arnett, January 19, 1982, OHTL. Arnett served as commissioner in Nome in 1952.

27. Ibid.; Boraas, citing Gerald E. Bowkett, *Reaching for a Star: The Final Campaign for Alaska Statehood* (Fairbanks: Epicenter Press, 1989), 6.

Chapter 7

1. John Hellenthal interviewed by the author May 15, 1982, OHTL.

2. Additional information on John McGinn is from the Alaska Mining Hall of Fame.

3. The population of Anchorage in 1940 was 4,229, and in 1950 it had risen to 11,254. Claus-M. Naske and Herman E. Slotnick, *Alaska: A History of the 49th State* (Grand Rapids, MI: William B. Eerdmans, 1979), appendix B, p. 305.

4. The US Army in Alaska (USARK), "The Army's Role in Building of Alaska," Pamphlet 360-5, Headquarters, US Army, Alaska, April, 1969. "World War II in Alaska; a historic and resources management plan: final report, U.S. Corps of Engineers, Alaska District, 1987." Information concerning the buildup in Anchorage is from these two publications, especially pages 2–11 of "World War II in Alaska," the US C.E.'s management plan.

5. Mary Childers Mangusso, "Anthony J. Dimond and the Politics of Integrity," in *An Alaska Anthology: Interpreting the Past*, ed. Stephen Haycox and Mary Childers Mangusso (Seattle: University of Washington Press, 1996), 246–66, at 249.

6. *U.S. v. Karl Drager*, November 25, 1942, Alaska Court Journal records, December 4, 1942–December 7, 1942.

7. The Davis and Renfrew firm evolved into the 1980s law firm Hughes, Thorsness, Gantz, Powell and Brundin. At that time the firm had sixty-one attorneys and offices in Juneau, Valdez, and Fairbanks, in addition to Anchorage. In the 1990s, the firm downsized to a single office in Anchorage with twenty-three attorneys (two, of counsel) and became known as Hughes Thorsness Powell Huddleston & Bauman. In 2016, the Anchorage firm is Hughes, Gorski, Seedorf, Odsen & Tervooren, with seven attorneys listed on its webpage.

8. Author interview with Mary Fasnacht Renfrew provided information on Davis and Renfrew partnership and personalities.

9. Terrence Cole and Elmer E. Rasmuson, *Banking on Alaska: The Story of The National Bank of Alaska*, vol. 2, *Elmer's Memoirs: Anecdotes and Vignettes of My 90 Years* (Anchorage: National Bank of Alaska; Rasmuson Foundation, 2000), 215. Rasmuson writes about Renfrew and also about the Davis and Renfrew law firm, pp. 279–80.

10. John Hughes arrived in Kodiak, Alaska, in 1940, where he drove a truck and worked in the cannery. He took the bar examination in 1946, passed in 1947, and started to practice law.

11. In the 1920s, R. E. Robertson served on a committee seeking the secession of the southeast from the rest of Alaska. The object was to allow the southeast to retain tax monies. Naske, *Alaska: A History of the 49th State*, 2nd ed., p. 140.

12. Senior Justice John Dimond interviewed by the author, April 21, 1981, OHTL, transcript, p. 24.

13. Retired Supreme Court Justice Buell Nesbett interviewed by the author, June 16, 1983, OHTL.

Chapter 8

1. Wendell Kay was interviewed by the author June 3, 1982, OHTL. Kay died in 1986. Information about Kay comes also from the *Alaska Bar Rag*, September 1979, p. 6, and his unpublished memoirs, located in the archives of the Anchorage Law Library.

2. Federal District Court Judge James Fitzgerald interviewed by the author, May 5, 1982. Fitzgerald was an assistant US attorney in the 1950s and practiced before Judge J. L. McCarrey Jr. in Anchorage.

3. Interview with John Rader by the author, OHTL, transcript, p. 13.

4. Kay memoir details the Allison case.

5. Letter of Roger Cremo to George Grigsby, November 20, 1961.

Chapter 9

1. Edgar Paul Boyko interviewed by the author, September 19, 1982, OHTL, transcript, pp. 38–39.

2. Ibid.

3. Information about capital punishment in territorial Alaska and George Folta comes from Averil Lerman, "The Trial and Hanging of Nelson Charles,"

Alaska Justice Forum 13, no. 1 (Spring 1996): 1, 8–12. An account based on historical research of the trial and execution for murder of a Native fisherman, Nelson Charles, in Juneau in 1939. This was one of the last executions in Alaska, which abolished the death penalty in 1957. The article looks at the circumstances surrounding the crime, the trial, and the execution. It also provides a list of where, when, and who was executed during the last century. One execution occurred in Nome in 1903, one in Sitka in 1921, two in Fairbanks in 1929, and three in Juneau, one in each of the following years: 1939, 1948, and 1950.

4. Anchorage Superior Court Justice Seaborn Buckalew interviewed by author, November 16, 1982, OHTL.

5. Ibid.

Chapter 10

1. Federal District Court Judge James Fitzgerald interviewed by author, May 5, 1982, OHTL. Information also from the foreword written by Judge Fitzgerald in *Down Darkness Wide: U.S. Marshals and the Last Frontier,* by James H. Chenoweth (Baltimore: Publish America, 2004).

2. See "Patrick J. Gilmore Jr.," obituary, *Ketchikan Daily News,* August 17, 1995, p. 2; "Gilmore Name a Part of Ketchikan," *Ketchikan Daily News,* August 21, 1995, p. 1.

3. "The former Chief of Police was known to, at times, carry four or five guns and other officers testified that his handling of these guns was homicidal. Several times he used these guns to threaten citizens and even police officers." Final Report of the Grand Jury for the Special October 1953 Term, Division Number One at Ketchikan, p. 3.

4. The grand jury alleged numerous counts of corruption within the Ketchikan Police Department, including police chief Del Freimuth's complicity with the Creek Street prostitution business, gambling businesses, and bootlegging. The grand jury found that the police not only tolerated the outlawed businesses but also frequented them, and in some cases protected them from planned raids. The grand jury also found that city officials were derelict in their duty to suppress vice and corruption. Final Report of the Grand Jury for the Special October 1953 Term, in Division Number One at Ketchikan. Filed January 7, 1954.

5. The grand jury report alleged Gilmore had been obstructing justice and recommended his removal. The allegations concerned Gilmore's failure to prosecute cases (not specifying which cases); that prostitutes got too light a fine in commissioner's court or weren't prosecuted vigorously; and that Gilmore's presentation to the grand jury was inadequate. Ibid., pp. 8–9.

6. See Averil Lerman material on Folta and death penalty cases in Alaska. Manuscript on file with the author.

Chapter 11

1. Arthur David Talbot interviewed by author, August 10, 1982, OHTL.

2. Boyko, OHTL.

3. Kim Rich, *Johnny's Girl: A Daughter's Memoir of Growing Up in Alaska's Underworld* (Portland, OR: Alaska Northwest Books, 1999). For a description of Eastchester Flats.

4. *Stringer*, 124 F. Supp. 705 (D. Alaska 1954), rev'd 233 F.2d 947 (9th Cir. 1956).

5. Kemp told Talbot that he had given Stringer $2,000 worth of promissory notes, in addition to $500 paid up front, to cover the legal fee in a white slavery case. The charges, arising from Kemp's alleged transportation of a prostitute from one bar to the next and picking up passengers who were potential clients, had been dismissed for lack of evidence.

6. *Stringer*, 124 F. Supp., at 706–13.

7. According to Talbot, the grand jury believed Talbot was covering up for Stringer: "From the evidence they heard they wanted to indict Herald for larceny by false pretenses." Even Talbot thought this was excessive and instead sent information to his boss, US Attorney Buckalew, charging Stringer with unprofessional conduct.

8. Senior US District Court Judge James M. Fitzgerald remembered being told by a US Justice Department official that John Manders did not pay his income tax. Manders was one of a number of people in territorial Alaska who balked at paying national taxes. Telephone interview with James M. Fitzgerald, Senior Judge, US District Court, November 1995.

9. As far as Fitzgerald could tell, Kemp had been unhappy with Stringer's fee and complained to his boss, the owner of his cab company, who allegedly told Kemp that the money must be going to take care of the judge. Telephone conversation with Judge Fitzgerald, November 1995.

11. Interview with James M. Fitzgerald, February 27, 1997.

12. *Stringer*, 124 F. Supp., at 707.

13. *United States v. Talbot*, 15 Alaska 590, 594 (1955).

14. Talbot told the court that Assistant US Attorney Clifford Groh and Buckalew refreshed his memory. Talbot then testified:

> When they tell me that they remember my saying such a thing it gives rise to grave doubt in my mind as to whether or not I said it, but if I said . . . it, I did not . . . remember having said it when I gave my answer on the stand, but it may very well be that my memory is faulty on that point and it is something that bothers me a good deal. I believe that if Mr. Buckalew had thought that I had seriously threatened to indict him that he would have fired me on the spot and yet we remained fast friends. *United States v. Talbot*, at 593.

15. *Stringer*, 124 F. Supp., at 716.

16. Id., at 715 (quoting People *ex rel.* Chicago Bar Ass'n v. Green 187 N.E. 811, 813 (Ill.1933)].

17. Fitzgerald interview, February 1997.

18. Boyko, OHTL.

19. Author telephone interview with Roger Cremo, December 26, 1995.

20. 1955 Alaska Sess. Laws 196. Passage of the Integrated Bar Act came too late to help Herald Stringer, whose case had already been appealed. *Stringer v. United States,* 233 F2d 947 (9th Cir. 1956).

21. Members of the first board of governors were Michael Monagle, John Connolly, James A. von der Heydt, Edward Davis, George B. Grigsby, Charles Clasby, Julien Hurley, Charles Cloudy, and Norman Banfield.

Chapter 12

1. Buell Nesbett interview, June 16, 1983, OHTL.

2. Examiners on Nesbett's exam included R. E. Robertson in Juneau and Warren Cuddy in Anchorage. Other examiners were in Nome and Fairbanks. Nesbett interview.

3. Interview with Clifford Groh Sr., February 23, 1982, OHTL.

4. Interview with Steven McCutcheon, OHTL.

5. According to Nesbett, Elmer Rasmuson alerted the banking board, which included his attorney, John Hughes, and used Hughes' influence with the board to get rid of Union Bank competition. Hughes said that this was not true and explained that he had been appointed to the territorial banking board through the recommendation of Marshall Crutcher, who owned the Bank of Kodiak. Hughes had been a member of the board of the Bank of Kodiak when he lived there. By the time he took a seat on the banking board he was no longer affiliated with that bank. Crutcher was the head of the banking board and one of the few certified public accountants in the territory.

"He was a pretty uptight fellow as far as accounting," Hughes said of Crutcher. He added that there were several territorial banks suspected of practices that were prejudicial to depositors. Hughes named the Bank of Cordova, the Crawford Bank, also known as Alaska Statebank, and the Union Bank, as doing business "on more generous terms than the Bank of Seattle." He added, "These practices that were mentioned and gossiped about were not criminal." Paperwork was a little less precise.

Hughes remembered hearing about at least one unorthodox practice at Union Bank. A teller told a person that his note was overdue. The person said he'd better see the bank manager since he didn't remember signing the note. The manager explained that yes, it wasn't that person's note, but that the manager had manufactured the note to keep the bank in balance. "No one got hurt by those things," Hughes said. But, he added, these loose practices did disturb the meticulous Marshall Crutcher.

Nesbett believed John Hughes did not want to be impressed by Seattle First's guarantee and worked to persuade other members of the board—who appeared to accept the assurance—to declare the bank in default. McCutcheon and Nesbett hired a private detective to follow John Hughes after the board meeting. The two men suspected that Rasmuson was behind the board's decision and their suspicions were confirmed, Nesbett concluded, when Hughes went directly to Elmer Rasmuson's house.

"We could only surmise what happened but we felt that [Hughes] was sent to that meeting to cause that decision to be made and had succeeded and rushed right out to tell Elmer, 'Man we got it. Got the Union Bank short.'"

Hughes, though, contested Nesbett's version. Hughes recalled that an accounting firm was asked to evaluate Union Bank and the firm would not give the banking board the assurances necessary to open the bank. It was only after Dan Cuddy of the First National Bank made representations that he would take over Union Bank's accounts, that Judge Dimond allowed the bank to reopen. Hughes did not dispute that he may have spoken with Elmer Rasmuson and told him about the banking board meeting. But, he added, Rasmuson and the National Bank of Alaska did not influence his position on the banking board. [Interview with John Hughes, April 9, 1997.]

6. Papers of Marcus Jensen, Folder 13, Folta letters, Alaska State Archives, Juneau, provided to author by Averil Lerman.

7. Interview with J. Gerald Williams, February 4, 1982, OHTL, pp. 16–17.

8. *Anchorage Times*, November 29, 1952, p. 1.

9. Gruening hired Nesbett and Wendell Kay to help in his suit against the *Juneau Daily Empire* in 1952, according to Nesbett.

Chapter 13

1. Clifford Groh Sr., interview with author, OHTL; Elmer Rasmuson memoir, pp. 287–90, on the firm; John Rader, interview with author, OHTL; Gordon Hartlieb interview with author, OHTL.

2. Jensen state archival file, newspaper stories and correspondence with Judge Folta regarding Warren Taylor.

3. Victor Fischer, *Alaska's Constitutional Convention* (Fairbanks: University of Alaska Press, 1975), 268, appendix D, "A Judiciary for Alaska."

4. Commentary from Constitutional Convention supporting Missouri Plan and outlining drawbacks of appointment and election of judges. http://www.ajc.state.ak.us/about/convmin.

5. Alaska Supreme Court Justice Warren W. Matthews (Ret.) presentation at the November 8, 2005, bar historian's luncheon commemorating the fiftieth anniversary of the Constitutional Convention, reprised on November 12, 2009,

as part of the Alaska Legal History Series commemorating the Fiftieth Anniversary of Statehood, November 9, 2009, draft.

6. Matthews presentation, 5–6.

7. Fischer, *Alaska's Constitutional Convention*, 113.

8. Nesbett, Davis, and Fitzgerald all became state court judges.

9. Discussion of this issue at the Constitutional Convention included the following exchange:

> V. RIVERS: I see that on the basis of area representation, the governing body of the organized state bar, not the membership shall select the appointees from the legal side. Is there some reason why these are not selected from the membership of the organized state bar, rather than by their governing body?
>
> MCLAUGHLIN: The intent was that there would be in existence or be created, a body which would be representative of all persons admitted to practice, and they would lay down the rules by which the governing body would designate people to the judicial council. It doesn't preclude election, it is determined on majority vote of the membership. The mechanics we felt should not be spelled out in the constitution.
>
> Alaska Legislative Council, Minutes of the Daily Proceedings, Alaska Constitutional Convention 731 (1965).

10. The Alaska Integrated Bar Act of 1955 created the Alaska Bar Association, a territory-wide association that governed the profession. Lawyers throughout Alaska elected representatives to sit on the board of governors. In 1959, the board of governors included the following: Wilfred C. Stump, president, Ketchikan; James A. von der Heydt, vice president, Nome; John R. Connolly, second vice president, Anchorage; Wendell P. Kay, secretary, Anchorage; William V. Boggess, Fairbanks; Clifford J. Groh, Anchorage; Robert L. Jernberg, Ketchikan; Robert McNealy, Fairbanks; and M. E. Monagle, Juneau. While the Alaska Bar Association and its board of governors began providing for territory-wide organization in 1955, lawyers continued to meet regularly at semiformal local bar association gatherings. The Juneau, Ketchikan, Anchorage, Valdez, Nome, and Tanana Valley Bar Associations had been in operation for many years prior to the passage of the Integrated Bar Act.

11. Ernie Bailey was Alaska Bar Association Board of Governor president, W. C. Stump's legal partner; Herald Stringer was board of governor member John Connolly's former legal partner.

12. Telephone interview with Fitzgerald, November 1995.

13. The following judges were appointed to the first state court bench: James A. von der Heydt, presiding judge, First District, Juneau; Walter E. Walsh, judge, First District, Ketchikan; Hubert A. Gilbert, presiding judge, Second District, Nome; Edward V. Davis, presiding judge, Third District, Anchorage; J. Earl Cooper, judge, Third District, Anchorage; James M. Fitzgerald, judge,

Third District, Anchorage; Everett W. Hepp, judge, Fourth District, Fairbanks. 1960 Alaska Session Laws VI.

14. Justice Walter H. Hodge, originally part of the Alaska Supreme Court, bought a house in Juneau, hoping that the court would be there. Justice Nesbett established Anchorage as the home of the Supreme Court. Hodge eventually applied for the federal court post and left the Supreme Court. Harry O. Arend was appointed to fill his seat on the Alaska Supreme Court.

Chapter 14

1. Clyde Coulter Houston, *Missoulian News*, June 24, 2007, http://missoulian. com/news/local/obituaries/01sun/clyde-coulter-houston/article_7a864db0-cc8e-5c38-a9c6-411150b047ae.html.

2. Alaska Bar Association, Minutes of the Board of Governors' Meeting (February 9, 1963), unpublished, on file with the Alaska Bar Association.

3. 378 P. 2d 644 (Alaska 1963).

4. Id., at 644.

5. Id., at 647.

6. Id., at 645.

7. Alaska Bar Association, Minutes of the Board of Governors' Meeting, March 11, 1963.

8. Ibid.

9. Senate Resolution 39, 3d Leg., 1st Session, 1963 Alaska Session Laws 162. The resolution read as follows:

> Whereas the Courts of many states, including the Supreme Court of the State of Alaska, have held that attorneys are officers of the court and their qualifications and fitness to practice law before the courts is a matter for final determination by the Supreme Court; and
>
> Whereas the Alaska Integrated Bar Act . . . raises the question of whether the Board of Governors of the Alaska Bar Association as presently constituted is a part of the executive or judicial branch of government;
>
> Be it resolved that the Supreme Court of the State of Alaska with the assistance of the Judicial Council and the Alaska Bar Association is respectfully requested to prepare suggested rules placing the Alaska Bar Association in the judicial branch of government and report its actions and recommendations, together with recommendations for any necessary legislative action consistent with its determinations, to the legislature at the time of the convening of the second session in 1964.

10. Interview with Burton Biss, December 30, 1983, Cravez, *Territorial Lawyers*.

11. Interview with Ret. Superior Court Judge Thomas Stewart, April 22, 1982, Cravez, *Territorial Lawyers*.

12. Alaska Bar Association, Minutes of the Board of Governors' Meeting, February 9, 1964.

13. Minutes of the Board of Governors' Meeting, May 7, 1964.

14. In re Supreme Court Orders No. 64, 68, 69, 70, and 71, 395 P.2d. 853 (Alaska 1964).

15. Interview with Kenneth R. Atkinson, Cravez, *Territorial Lawyers*.

16. In a 1964 newspaper article, Alaska bar president Robert Ziegler was reported to have said that the court apparently took this action as a result of a poll among the board of governors in which, "we had a choice of being hung or poisoned. The unilateral action of the Supreme Court either jeopardizes or destroys the Alaska Bar Association as legislatively constituted. I regret very much the fact that the Supreme Court has taken the action that it has. And I doubt there can be found within the state of Alaska nine attorneys who will voluntarily serve on a re-constituted board of governors."

17. "Bar Funds Taken at Gun Point," *Anchorage Times*, July 24, 1964, p. 1.

18. Telephone interview with Roger Cremo, December 26, 1995.

19. Letter from Nesbett to McNealy, July 24, 1964.

20. Chief Justice Buell Nesbett, press release, July 29, 1964. Press release can be found in closed case file for *Alaska Bar Assn v. Nesbett*, No. A-42-64 CIV. (D. Alaska filed July 29, 1964) on file with the US District Court, D. Alaska.

21. Interview with Robert Ziegler, April 20, 1982, Cravez, *Territorial Lawyers*.

22. Ziegler wrote: "Inasmuch as both parties are represented by counsel that counsel should have been consulted and a stipulation entered into by and between counsel encompassing whatever points contained in Order No. 72 that counsel could agree upon." Letter from Alaska Bar President Robert Ziegler to Chief Justice Buell Nesbett, September 10, 1964.

23. Interview with Atkinson, Cravez, *Territorial Lawyers*.

24. Deposition of Harland W. Davis, *In re Alaska Supreme Court Orders* (No. 532).

Chapter 15

1. Tom Brennan, *Cold Crime: How Police Detectives Solved Alaska's Most Sensational Cases* (Kenmore, WA: Epicenter Press, 2005).

2. Ibid., 125.

3. The mediation team included Dean Alfred J. Schweppe of the University of Washington Law School, Oregon Supreme Court Justice William M. McAllister, and Washington Supreme Court Justice Hugh J. Rosellini.

4. Letter from Arthur David Talbot to Walter H. Hodge, Judge US District Court, December 23, 1964.

5. "Talbot Is Ousted from Bar Case," *Anchorage Daily News*, February 24, 1965, p. 1.

6. Ibid.

7. Interview with Boyko, OHTL.

Chapter 16

1. Grace Berg Schaible interviewed by the author October 3, 1983, OHTL. Telephone interview with Schaible, April 8, 1997.

2. Barbara Hood, profile of M. Ashley Dickerson prepared for the "1998 Women in Alaska Law" Archive, based on an interview with Ms. Dickerson on March 26, 1998.

3. Ibid.

4. Telephone conversation with Leroy Baker, 2016.

5. Julia O'Malley, article on Ashley Dickerson, quoting Justice Dana Fabe, *Anchorage Daily News*, February 21, 2007, upon Ms. Dickerson's death.

Chapter 17

1. Rabinowitz, oral history, 2000.

Afterword

1. Author meeting with Russell Arnett, summer 1980.

2. Russell Arnett, interviewed by author, January 19, 1982, OHTL.

Index